WE'LL BE IN YOUR MOUNTAINS,
WE'LL BE IN YOUR SONGS

WE'LL BE IN YOUR MOUNTAINS, WE'LL BE IN YOUR SONGS

A Navajo Woman Sings

ELLEN McCULLOUGH-BRABSON
and
MARILYN HELP

Foreword by David P. McAllester

University of New Mexico Press
Albuquerque

Library of Congress Cataloging-in-Publication Data

McCullough-Brabson, Ellen.
    We'll be in your mountains, we'll be in your songs : a Navajo woman
sings / Ellen McCullough-Brabson and Marilyn Help ; foreword by David P.
McAllester.— 1st ed.
        p.   cm.
Includes bibliographical references (p.   ), discography (p.   ), and
videography (p.   ).
        ISBN 0-8263-2217-4 (cloth : alk. paper)
        1. Folk songs, Navajo—History and criticism. 2. Navajo Indians—Music—
History and criticism. 3. Help, Marilyn, 1956– I.
Help, Marilyn, 1956– II. Title.
ML3557 .M36 2001
782.42'162972—DC21

                                                                    00-012571

The Laser Navajo™ Palatino font used to print this work is available from Linquist's Software, Inc.,
PO Box 580, Edmonds, WA 98020-0580 USA tel (425) 775-1130 www.linguistsoftware.com.

Frontispiece:

Marilyn Help, Miss Navajo Nation, 1977–78. Photographer unknown.

The Navajo way is a good way to live. I am teaching my children the same things my grandmother taught me, about the Holy People and Navajo life.

—*Marilyn Help*

We'll be in your mountains, we'll be in your songs . . . that's how you will remember us and our teachings so that you may have a good life.

—*The Holy People, when they gave music to the Diné*

Contents

Illustrations

Acknowledgments

To my parents, my children, Mother Earth, Father Sky, and all the Holy People.

Marilyn Help

To my family, for support and love, and my Navajo friends, especially Ruth Roessel, for inspiration. . . as we learn more about each other, may we joyously pass the "cultural baton" throughout the centuries.

Ellen McCullough-Brabson

Foreword

A happy combination of interests resulted in *We'll Be in Your Mountains, We'll Be in Your Songs: A Navajo Woman Sings* (the first part of the title is taken from what the gods told the Navajo people). Ellen McCullough-Brabson, a professor of music at the University of New Mexico, and Marilyn Help, a Navajo teacher of unusual imagination and breadth of experience, met by chance, developed a deep friendship, and persevered during many years of mutual support to bring their book into existence. Their achievement would not have been possible without the willing involvement of their families as well. Marilyn's parents and children are present everywhere in these pages as part of the story and in the many photographs that enrich the text. John M. Brabson, an engineer and computer scientist, has had a love affair with the book as he cheered on the authors and devoted long hours of proofreading to the project in its writing and rewriting.

In the history of European American and Native American relations, the Navajos were relatively isolated from the usual conquest, despoliation, and infection with new diseases that devastated so many Native communities. Kit Carson's campaign in 1867 was a "scorched earth" event rather than a massacre, and the incarcer-ation at Fort Sumner, hard though it was, ended in a few years after Congress discovered how ineffectual and costly it was. The People were allowed to return to their lands with livestock and equipment for a new start in the way of life they had already developed. The result was a consolidation of what had become "traditional" Navajo culture. Washington Matthews, an army surgeon stationed in the Navajo country in the 1880s and 1890s, astonished the outside world with his insightful reports on Navajo arts and their unique philosophical and religious concept of the universe. Artists and scholars of every kind visited the Navajos to record the way of life of this largest of the North American communities. The concluding phrase of many Navajo prayers, "With beauty all around me, I shall walk in beauty!" has captured the imagination of readers ever since it was translated and published by Matthews.

Why, then, produce still another book and add it to the many hundreds already published on the Navajos? For one thing, Navajo culture is one of continual growth and development: there is never a "last word" on its content. And there has never been a point of view quite like this collaboration between Marilyn Help and Ellen McCullough-Brabson. Marilyn, a teacher and home-keeper for a large family, is known across the huge reservation (more than three times the size of Massachusetts) for her talents, her outgoing personality, and her firm adherence to the Navajo ideals of self-reliance and harmonious relations with the natural world. Ellen, a sensitive musician with an unusual appreciation for the modalities of musics outside her own culture, enables Marilyn to express her own responses to the music of her people.

The songs, presented in impressive depth, were carefully chosen to represent some of the principal facets of Navajo life. The book avoids any venture into the sacred songs of the great ceremonial chants, but each chapter is constructed around a different genre of the more secular music, in the context of Marilyn's perspectives and reminiscences on what the songs mean to her. A special treat for the reader is the accompanying recording in her full, buoyant voice, so that each song comes alive aurally, while the transcriptions of music and text enable the reader to follow, learn, and remember. Marilyn has taught these delightful songs to the many Navajo children and teachers who have attended her classes. Each song, presented in such unusual detail, is a lesson in Navajo culture and a gift from these resilient people.

I consider this book to be a treasure. It is the result of a long friendship across cultural barriers to taste the pleasures of mutual discovery, and it enables the reader (and listener!) to participate in this experience.

David P. McAllester
Professor Emeritus
of Music and Anthropology
Wesleyan University

Preface

My first contact with the Diné, the Navajo people, was over thirty years ago, when my family and I traveled from Ohio to Tucson, Arizona, to visit our relatives. Since this was our first time in the area, we decided to take the scenic route through Mesa Verde National Monument. After an impressive tour of this historical site, we ventured onward through breathtaking Monument Valley, a famous part of the Navajo Nation. Little did we know as we journeyed toward Tucson that our car engine was gradually burning out due to a faulty oil change. The mechanic at the gas station in Mesa Verde had changed our oil but hadn't replaced the oil plug. As a result our burned-out car stopped dead in the middle of the Navajo Nation, several miles outside Kayenta, Arizona. Fortunately, the Navajo tribal police soon came by to assist us. They looked in the back part of our station wagon and saw my ten-year-old sister playing cards by herself. With a twinkle in their eyes, they quickly said, "You better watch out! There are Indians around here!" and heartily laughed. We admired their ability to tease us and to help us make the most of a dismal situation. These officers planted the first cultural seed, compelling me to learn more about the Diné.

Who would have imagined then that many years later I would be a music professor teaching at the University of New Mexico in Albuquerque, a city just a few hours away from Dinétah, Navajoland? Because of the proximity of the university to the Navajo Nation, I have had the rich opportunity to teach and work with talented Navajo students, like Marilyn Help, coauthor of this book.

Marilyn was a student in my class several years ago. I was impressed with her maturity and insight into traditional Diné ways, her willingness to share her culture, and her lovely singing voice. At the end of the semester she invited me to visit her at her parents' home on the Navajo Nation. A year later my family and I decided to take up her offer. Although we tried quite valiantly to find her home across miles of open mesas and arroyos, we got hopelessly lost on the way to her hogan. There we were, a white family, in a white car, in the Navajo Nation many miles outside of Gallup, searching for a former student I hadn't seen for a year. In the distance we saw a Navajo man standing outside his home. We turned into his driveway and asked this Navajo elder if he knew John C. Help, Marilyn's father. The Navajo Holy People must have smiled upon us because he replied, "I am John C. Help," and he immediately went to

Marilyn's hogan to alert her that guests had arrived. Although I had written her a letter about our upcoming visit, Marilyn was stunned when she saw me. She hugged me warmly and then spontaneously took off the purple squash blossom necklace that she was wearing around her neck and graciously placed it on mine as a gift of welcome. Marilyn was thrilled that we had found her, the first white folks ever to visit her home. But most important, she and I both rejoiced because we felt a powerful cultural connection, a friendship that celebrates difference.

After several other visits, I approached Marilyn about collaborating with me on a collection of Navajo social songs that would be appropriate for non-Navajos to sing. Although there were numerous tapes available that featured Navajo music and many books that examined Navajo culture, very few sources contained the musical notation for Navajo social songs. With rare exceptions, those that were accessible had limited or no information on the cultural context of the music. Thus the project *We'll Be in Your Mountains, We'll Be in Your Songs: A Navajo Woman Sings* was born. Our selection of music is limited to twelve songs in order to provide the depth and detail that give a rich, resonant explanation of the cultural meaning of the music. Each chapter presents an aspect of Navajo culture that is augmented by a traditional or contemporary Navajo social song. We intentionally omitted the large repertoire of ceremonial music, such as songs about the creation story, hogans, and weaving, because of their sacredness.

The book and accompanying recording are designed for people of all ages and in all walks of life who want to celebrate Navajo music and culture. It must be emphasized that this book was written with great respect for the Navajos and for the Holy People. Although the music selected for this book is secular in nature, these songs and dances, whether traditional or contemporary, are ultimately gifts from the Holy People. Therefore each song must be performed with respect for its particular meaning and context.

"The corn pollen rule" is a popular expression used by Navajos. It roughly translates as, "Follow your traditional ways," or, "Follow the teachings of your elders." This book and tape are meant to do just that. They celebrate Navajo culture through music. In addition, *We'll Be in Your Mountains, We'll Be in Your Songs* offers insight via the direct quotations of Marilyn Help as to what it is like to be a contemporary Navajo woman. She gracefully balances living in a culturally diverse society with her role as a culture bearer for her traditional Navajo ways. Through the twelve Navajo songs presented here in their cultural context, Marilyn Help passes a cultural baton to her children and her children's children and to all people. She honors "the corn pollen rule" with the beauty of her thoughts and her songs.

Ellen McCullough-Brabson
Professor of Music
The University of New Mexico

Chapter 1

THE VOICE OF MARILYN HELP: A NAVAJO WOMAN SINGS

The Song . . .

"Jóó Ashílá"
(Traveling Together)

One of the most frequently quoted and poignantly powerful Navajo litanies is the Navajo prayer of beauty.

> Beauty before me I walk
> Beauty behind me I walk
> Beauty above me I walk
> Beauty below me I walk
> Beauty all about me I walk
> In beauty all is made whole
> In beauty all is restored.*
> —Shonto Begay,
> *Navajo Visions and Voices across the Mesa*

*(*This litany is the concluding formula in many of the Navajo Blessingway prayers.)*

The spirit of beauty projected in this part of traditional Navajo prayer resonates perfectly in Marilyn Help, a contemporary Navajo woman who walks in *hózhǫ́*, the Navajo word for beauty, peace, and harmony. She balances the constant yet changing influences of the dominant European American culture with the teachings of the Holy People, the Navajo deities who created the Diné, the People. Marilyn lives, shares, and teaches traditional Navajo culture to her children and the students at the school where she works with commitment and determination. Although she identifies strongly with the personification "I am an American," she maintains and celebrates her Navajo culture, too. She passionately cares about the Diné, her people, and their traditional and contemporary culture. (see Plate 1)

Her strong sense of cultural identity is exemplified every time she greets someone new. She introduces herself in the traditional Navajo way, which includes stating her given name as well as the clans of her parents: "I am Marilyn Hood, born of Bitter Water Clan and born for Yucca Fruit Strung in a Line Clan. My maternal grandfather's clan is Darkened with the Charcoal Streaked Red Running into the Water, and my paternal grandfather's clan is Black Streaked Wood." Her acknowledgment of her clan connections permits other Navajos to track her genealogy and discover whether or not they belong to the same clan, allowing them to treat each other as "relatives." If Navajos are related to each other by clan, they may call each other "my sister," "my mother," or "my grand-father" even if they are not blood relatives.

She was given the English name Marilyn by her parents, who teasingly said that she was named after one of her father's old girlfriends. Her parents also affectionately gave her a Navajo name, Ooshii, which means "thin one." Marilyn's maiden name, Help, was given to her paternal grandfather years ago by European American neighbors because he was so generous and helpful to everyone. His original Navajo name was Tsi' naajinii Yidlohígíí biye' (Black Streaked Wood Laughing). Her father, John C. Help, also has a traditional name, Tsi' naajinii Yidlohígíí biye' bitsii' agodígíí, which means "Son of the Black Streaked Wood Laughing. His Hair Is Cut Off." (see Figure 1)

Born in Fort Defiance, Arizona, and raised in Tolakai, New Mexico, Marilyn was one of nine children. She and her five sisters (Sandra, Barbara, Leila, Doris, and Karen) and three brothers (Leonard, Calvin, and Brian) were raised in both traditional and contemporary ways. Marilyn learned about Navajo culture from her grandmother and father, powerful influences in her life. But because her mother wanted her to fit in with the dominant culture, Marilyn also learned the ways of the *bilagáana*, or white man. When she was growing up, her family lived in a hogan at Tolakai on the Navajo Nation.

Figure 1
Grace and John C. Help, Marilyn Help's parents. All photographs are by coauthor Ellen McCullough-Brabson unless otherwise noted.

Although their hogan eventually got electricity, there was no running water; it was carried from the nearby water hole. Marilyn remembers this daily chore of hauling water with her sisters.

We used to have to carry water from the water hole that was on the south side of our place where the big rock sits. I remember going up there when it was like a pond; water was always in there. Sometimes in the afternoon there would be bugs sitting on it, and you would have to move the water dipper to clean around the area, then you would put the water into the dipper and put it into the jugs. My sisters and I did that in the morning and the afternoon. We would use the water to wash dishes, diapers, and clothes as well as for our drinking water and cooking. The water jug was a big barrel water cooler. It was quite heavy, and we would need two of us to carry it, one on one side and one on the other. We would walk a few steps and then rest for a while, and then we would take a few steps more.

The pond was less than half a mile from our hogan and was the same watering hole that we used for our livestock. We knew that the best time to get the water was early in the morning when nobody was herding sheep. Then the water was clear and perfect to use for drinking.

Marilyn's preschool years alternated between living with her parents and staying with her grandmother on her father's side, her *nálí*. She spent many summers of her youth with her grandmother and acknowledged that the significant seeds of traditional Navajo culture were planted during that time. Her grandmother lived in Leupp, Arizona, a small town between Winslow and Flagstaff. Although Marilyn loved and respected her very much, she remembers how homesick she used to get for her parents and family.

When I used to visit my grandmother for the summer, I would feel bad because I did not want my parents to leave me. But after a while I got used to her place, and then I would like it. I used to sleep by my grandma, just the two of us, side by side in her hogan, on a sheepskin at night. She would get up early in the morning and start singing her songs. And then she would tell me to get up and go outside and greet the Holy People.

Although she let me know when she was disappointed, she never said a harsh word to me. Instead she would say, "This is what I didn't like, my child." I would be so hurt and feel so bad that I would want to cry. I wanted to please my grandmother more than anything because I respected her and loved her so much. She taught me many things about Navajo life. When I was really little, she tried to teach me how to make bread and biscuits. I would try really hard to do what she said, but my biscuits would turn out so ugly. Instead of complaining about them, my grandmother would eat them and say, "This is good." I really loved her for that.

Although Marilyn herded sheep frequently when she was a young girl, she did have some time to play with toys that she created from the natural environment. For example, when she stayed at her grandmother's hogan, she used sheep droppings, *dibé bichaan*, to mold animal shapes. In addition, she collected rocks with interesting shapes to use as make-believe horses and other animals. She used sticks for her "play people." And when there was a summer rain, Marilyn would use the mud that curled up in the arroyo to create tables, chairs, and trucks. During one Christmas season Marilyn was given a bilagáana, or "white," doll from the church. She remembers carrying her doll around all over the place and wrapping it up, washing its hair and body, and changing its diaper.

When Marilyn was five, she went to Twin Lakes Boarding School. She recalled that she could hardly speak any English at the time. Marilyn remembers her first day of school, when all of the new children were sent to the beginners' room, where the Navajo cook, a school employee who spoke fluent Navajo, tried to explain the fire alarm system to the new students. The cook said, "When you hear the fire bell ring, line up in an orderly fashion and then quietly and quickly walk outside." Marilyn was quite frightened when the cook started to talk about the fire alarm; she was afraid that the school would burn

and that she would be trapped inside and never see her parents again. The other children must have been afraid, too, because when the bell rang for them to practice the fire drill, they all ran out of the door hysterically and had to try it again and again. Marilyn chides that if they had just not been so frightened, they would have done it right the first time.

Although Marilyn would have preferred to live at home with her parents, she had to stay at the boarding school for two weeks at a time. She was assigned a bunk and a cubbyhole that she used to store her clothes. A night attendant washed her dirty laundry and selected a clean outfit for her to wear each day. She vividly remembers the offensive smell of ink that was used to mark and identify each child's clothes. Marilyn's parents literally had to drag her tearfully to school after each break.

In her later elementary school years, Marilyn changed schools and went to Chuska, a Bureau of Indian Affairs (BIA) school. Although Marilyn's native tongue was Navajo, she was forbidden to speak it at her new school. Like other educational institutions designed to educate Native Americans during the late nineteenth and early twentieth century, the main focus of the curriculum was to acculturate Native Americans to white society. The use of native languages was frequently forbidden, as well as adherence to other traditional customs. Marilyn reminisces about the times she disobeyed and spoke her native tongue anyway.

When we got to Chuska, we were told

Figure 2
Marilyn Help and four of her children
(clockwise, starting from the left),
Lyle, Shannon, Joni, and Warren.
Photographer unknown.

to only speak English, not Navajo. The teachers said, "You're going to have to quit talking Navajo. If you're caught talking Navajo, then you're going to have to scrub the rest room with a toothbrush." Even though they said that, I got caught speaking Navajo several times. One time as my punishment I had to write "I will not talk Navajo" three or four hundred times. I was only a little girl, and it was so hard to do. My hand got very tired, although I tried really, really hard. My writing got pretty horrible at the end. And in third

or fourth grade I got my mouth washed out with soap for speaking Navajo. I don't know why they did that to us because it was really crazy.

We were also forbidden to attend our ceremonials. If we wanted to go to one, we had to sneak away. We made up stories and gave excuses in order to get out and go to them. But now they let you do it.

When Marilyn was in fifth grade, she transferred to Tohatchi Public Schools, where she stayed through her senior year, graduating with her high school diploma. She then attended Brigham Young University for two years and received an associate of arts degree. Although she wanted to continue her college education, she decided to work for a while to earn money so that she could eventually return to the university. It was during this period that she entered several beauty pageants, a desire that she'd had in high school but was unable to fulfill.

Her first title was Miss Santa Fe Safety Queen. She had to compete in both the modern and traditional categories in order to win this crown. She dressed in contemporary clothes and spoke in English for the modern category and wore her Navajo regalia and sang a Navajo song for the traditional part. Marilyn discovered that competing in a beauty pageant was an excellent learning experience because it motivated her to speak to people without getting embarrassed or acting shy in front of a microphone. It also gave her a strong self-concept and nurtured her self-esteem. She eventually reigned as

Figure 3
Marilyn Help's hogan at her home in Tolakai, New Mexico.

Miss Navajo, Miss Navajo Nation Rodeo Cowboys Association, and Miss Navajo Fort Defiance. In fact, she occasionally held two titles at the same time, a feat that the beauty pageant organizers have since ruled as impermissible. Marilyn describes the Miss Navajo competition:

> For the modern category of Miss Navajo, I demonstrated painting and sculpturing and sang a song. And for the traditional category I illustrated corn grinding, sang a corn-grinding song, and performed several cere-monialsongs. In addition, I showed how to wrap the intestine of a sheep for cooking. I put a lot of effort into the event, and I won the title.

Marilyn's two daughters, Shannon (born in 1981) and Joni (born in 1984), have fol-

lowed in their mother's footsteps. Although Joni isn't very interested in competing in beauty pageants, Shannon has already been crowned Miss Navajo Nation Rodeo Cowboys Association, just like her mother. (see Plate 2)

Soon after Marilyn received her beauty pageant titles, she got married in a traditional Navajo wedding ceremony performed by her father. Marilyn has four children, Shannon, Lyle, Joni, and Warren, who are born of Bitter Water Clan and born for Towering House Clan. Her fifth child, Shane (born in 1991), is born of Bitter Water Clan and born for Paiute Red Running into Water Clan. Her husband passed away in 1988, which left her a widow to raise her children as a single parent. During her marriage she strayed from her traditional ways because her husband did not support the Diné way of life. However, after his death she turned back to her native culture and pursued her dream of becoming a teacher. She completed her elementary education degree at the University of New Mexico (UNM) in Albuquerque and the UNM Gallup branch near her home, no small feat for a single mother with five children. Her only regret during this period was that she was forced to send her children to boarding school at Fort Wingate during part of that time. Marilyn is currently the Navajo culture teacher at the Ch'ooshga Community School in Tohatchi, New Mexico. (see Figure 2)

Marilyn and her children live in the checkerboard area of the Navajo Nation outside of Gallup, New Mexico. The term "checkerboard" refers to land that the Diné claimed as their own until the U.S. government arbitrarily divided it between the Navajos, railroad companies, and ranchers. The intent of the checkerboard land distribution was to encourage railroad transportation and American expansion in the Southwest and West. Marilyn's home is a modest cinder block and wood house next to her father's house. Her family has a traditional hogan on their property that is used mainly for ceremonies and storage. Although Marilyn could move to more convenient housing, she and her children prefer to live a traditional Navajo lifestyle. As with many Navajos, their livestock (horses and sheep) live on their property with them. Even though they have electricity in their home, just as it was when Marilyn was a child, they don't have water and must replenish their supply several times a week. (see Figure 3)

We go to a well that is about six miles

to the north of our house about three days each week. A windmill supplies the water. Because it is available for public access, we are allowed to use it. Since we have livestock, we take a lot of water each week. We usually fill up six big water barrels each time we go. When you haul water in your truck, you leave the barrels in the truck bed and connect a hose to the water faucet. Then you fill up one water barrel at a time. Once you get home, you attach another hose and put it into the water trough. The barrels stay on the truck.

When we bathe, we take what we call a "birdbath" or "sponge bath." Since we don't have a shower, we have learned to get used to bathing this way and washing our hair in a pan. We use the same water that we wash our hair in to bathe with, too.

Marilyn's home has an electric stove, a refrigerator, a television, and a VCR, as well as a wood-burning stove to heat their house in the winter.

A primary goal of Marilyn's child-rearing philosophy is for her children to appreciate and understand traditional Navajo culture. Marilyn has told them the Navajo creation story; described the Holy People; explained the ceremonies; nurtured their understanding of customs, foods, and lifestyle; and celebrated her joy in being Navajo.

I choose to live where I live because I want my children to grow up in a traditional Navajo way. They need to take care of their animals and appreciate Mother Earth. I want them to grow up with the same values that I was brought up with so that they will be able to share what they know with their children. I tell them to pray for themselves and their future. The Navajo way is a good way to live. I am teaching my children the same things my grandmother taught me, about the Holy People and Navajo life.

An integral component of Marilyn's parenting skills is the sharing of Navajo songs and dances. She is constantly singing traditional and contemporary Navajo music to her children. Whether in her home or her truck, Marilyn's voice can be heard as she lives her culture through song.

The Song Connection

"Jóó Ashílá" captures the spirit of Marilyn and her family "traveling together" as they express the familiar Navajo sentiment "happy about beauty." This song illustrates the complexity of the Navajo language and celebrates traditional Navajo culture as it is explained and sung by the voice of Marilyn Help.

"Jóó Ashílá"
(Traveling Together)

Background Information

I learned this song from my dad when I was a little girl. He always used to sing this song for us when we were growing up. It is sung at the Squaw Dance or Enemyway. You can dance to it, too, and more lyrics can be added to it. But this is the real simple form that I learned from my dad, the way he taught me. "Jóó Ashílá" means "walking together, traveling together." It is a song that you can sing while you are driving and traveling together. My children know this song very well. I have also taught this song to my kids at school. My dad taught it to us when we were in our hogan. Sometimes he would tell us the dance and he would be drumming and then we would be dancing and walking in a circle in the hogan. We did not have TV or radio, so this is how we would keep ourselves occupied. This is the way that it was.

"Jóó Ashílá" is a social song. I think it is a very old song because it has been sung at the Squaw Dances, at the Enemyway, and then also just sung at home.

"Jóó Ashílá" is a traditional Navajo social

song and part of the Squaw Dance repertoire. This genre of music includes a wide variety of song types that the Diné sing at the Enemyway ceremony. Through an elaborate production of songs and dances performed for purification and protection, this popular three-day ritual heals the patient, the "one sung over." The Diné believe that the Enemyway cleanses and restores balance to a Navajo who has had too much contact with the outside world. It was originally performed for warriors who had just returned from battle in order to prevent the ghosts of their enemies from haunting them (Kluckhohn and Leighton 1974, 222). Armed service personnel often participate in an Enemyway after they come back from their tour of duty, as well as former hospital patients who purify themselves from their exposure to "ghosts" from non-Navajos recently deceased (McAllester 1992, 38). The Diné conduct the Enemyway only during the late spring, summer, and early fall; to do otherwise is taboo, although occasionally an exception has been made by special arrangement.

Squaw Dance songs are the social part of the Enemyway ceremony, and outsiders, non-Navajos, may observe and even join in the dancing. The Squaw Dance repertoire includes Sway, Gift, Circle, Two-step, and Skip songs. Even though the designation Squaw Dance suggests that each of these song types includes dancing, that is not the case. Singers perform the Sway and Gift songs without dancing to them. In addition, each category of songs has a set order of performance during the Enemyway ceremony.

Sway songs precede the Two-step and Skip songs every time the Diné sing them in the ceremony. They perform the Gift songs only on the second and third morning of the Enemyway. The Circle Dance occurs during the late afternoon of the third day of the ritual (McAllester 1992, 39–41). Singers usually accompany the Squaw Dance songs on a small water drum. This instrument's resonating chamber is a container, such as a small clay pot, that is partially filled with water. The drummer uses the water from the resonating chamber to wet the drumhead, thus producing a distinctive, warm sound. Because of its sacredness and healing power, many Navajos perform with the water drum only in ceremonial context. Marilyn honors this tradition and does not accompany her songs with a water drum.

Although the term Squaw Dance infers that only women participate, both men and women perform the dances during this social part of the Enemyway. Navajo tradition dictates that women choose men as partners for the Two-step and Skip music at the ceremony. This ritual underscores the prominence of women in Diné culture. According to McAllester, "It is always 'ladies choice,' a reflection, perhaps, of the powerful position women have in Navajo society. They own the household; the children belong to the mother's clan, not the father's; and when a couple marries it is traditional for the husband to move in with his wife's family" (McAllester 1992, 39). After the dance the man must pay the woman a small amount of money, such as a dime, quarter, or dollar, for this honor. McAllester states that this tradition is a carryover from one of Monster Slayer's adventures: "This is a symbol of the war booty brought back by Enemy Slayer from a mythical war and given away to Navajo girls in the story in celebration of the victory" (McAllester 1992, 39). According to Marilyn, it's not unusual for some Navajo men to "hide" in their trucks when the dancing starts so that they won't be asked to dance. She also says that her sons accept dance invitations at the Enemyway because she makes them do it. Of course, other men like to dance and start jingling the coins in their pockets in anticipation (Roseann Willink, personal communication, 1997). This well-known three-day ceremony provides a forum for festivity and socialization. The Enemyway ceremony is so popular that a spin-off has developed from it—the Navajo Song and Dance Contest.

The Navajo Song and Dance Contest is simultaneously a colorful spectacle and controversial social event developed by the Navajos during the last decade and a half. It is a competition that features singers and dancers who perform selected Squaw Dance music (the Two-step and Skip) taken from the Enemyway ceremony. Many Diné participate in the contest and support its concept; however, some traditional Navajos question whether or not songs and dances should be taken from the Enemyway ceremony, a ritual traditionally performed between the first thunder of spring and the first frost of winter, and turned into a contest format that may occur anytime during the year. Marilyn believes that the Song and Dance Contests should be held only during the appropriate

seasons, conforming to the time strictures for the Enemyway. She states:

> Sometimes I sing in the Song and Dance Contests. I only go during the spring and summertime. I do not go in the wintertime because it is not supposed to be done during the winter. But yet, it is done. A lot of the medicine people say we should not even have Song and Dance Contests in the winter. It should not be done because it confuses the Holy People. They will hear it. The medicine people say that this could be the reason why our weather has been really acting up.

Although traditional Diné, like Marilyn, participate in the Song and Dance Contests only during the appropriate months, it is a popular fund-raiser on the Navajo Nation and still occurs year-round, despite the controversy over its use. Prizes are given to the best dancers and singers and include such rewards as trophies and grocery money. Marilyn, who has won several first-place singing awards in this event, gives her opinion regarding the criteria for the winners of the music performers, who may be male or female.

> Sometimes it's really funny, the words that they produce. You know, the men that sing together out there; it's really funny, you laugh. You laugh and think, "It's a cute one, I like that one." You listen to the group.
> There are certain groups that keep up

a good rhythm and good beat and loud singing. Those are the ones that sing really, really good. And sometimes you think, "Oh, this group should win." They do win sometimes. Loud singing and keeping together and having a good rhythm or beat are the criteria for winning.

Marilyn notes that there is some confusion regarding the terms *Two-step* and *Skip*. She states that the Navajos she knows in Arizona and New Mexico often interchange the terms for the dances. Although the tempo of the drumbeat ultimately determines the dance step, the words used to describe the performance depend on the locale. In this text the Two-step refers to the dance step that requires the dancers to lift their feet upward in a sprightly manner as they move to the beat. The Skip refers to the step dancers perform with a heel-toe, toe-heel, or exaggerated "skip" movement.

The use of the terms *Circle Dance* and *Round Dance* is also inconsistent. McAllester refers to the music that the Diné perform at the Enemyway during the afternoon of the third day as "Circle Dance" songs. However, some of my Navajo informants call these songs the "Round Dance." To avoid confusion, the term Circle Dance is used.

Since many of the songs in this book are social songs that are part of the Squaw Dance repertoire, the authors sincerely desire that readers of this book honor the time strictures for the performance of these songs and their corresponding dances. The

discussion and analysis of the music at the end of every chapter gives information about the appropriate time for each song and dance performance.

Information about the music

"Jóó Ashílá" illustrates many of the musical characteristics prominent in Navajo music as outlined by McAllester and Mitchell in chapter 7 of this book, "Music of the Diné." Marilyn accompanies "Jóó Ashílá," as well as the other songs in this book, with a large "Pueblo-style" drum that her brother gave her family. The resonating chamber of the drum is a series of strips of wood stapled together. Deer hide stretches tightly over the open ends. Marilyn's drumstick head is deer hide, too. The drum provides a steady, recurring accompaniment for the song. Vocables, words that do not have a translation but are integral to the meaning of the song, occur at the beginning, in interludes between the translatable text, and at the end. The melody, which outlines a triad, starts low, then leaps upward to the next octave. Each of the vocable patterns sounds on the tonic, or "home" tone. Although the beat is consistent throughout the song, the meter is not. Changing meters accommodate the text of the song. Quarter notes and eighth notes are the predominant note values. (see Plate 3)

Experiencing the music

Since the Diné transmit their songs aurally, the traditional way to learn "Jóó Ashílá" is to listen to it again and again until it is "in your ear." As Marilyn says, "If you get it in your ear quickly, it was 'meant to be.'" Once the melody is familiar, practice the words repeatedly. The beat is compelling and beckons dancers to join in with the Two-step. Women choose a male partner, then the couple stands side by side, with the male on the outside of the circle, and joins hands or hooks elbows. In some cases, the female partner may even grab the male's shirt as they move around the circle. Both partners face forward and dance clockwise around the circle. They move to the beat by lifting their feet in a sprightly manner, alternating between their left foot and right foot. It does not matter which foot the partners choose to begin the dance, as long as they both start with the same foot. If there is a shortage of male dancers, two or three female dancers perform the Two-step together or one male between two females may dance together. The Diné traditionally perform "Jóó Ashílá" during the spring, summer, and early fall.

Because the music of the Navajo passes from one generation to the next by oral tradition, there is no standardized system for its transcription. Thus there are many choices for how to present Navajo songs using Western notation. In fact, there are probably as many possibilities for how to transcribe Navajo music as there are musicians who could write them. Since the intent of this book is for the reader to learn the songs by oral tradition from listening to the accompanying recording, we chose to present a simple and user-friendly sketch of the music. The musical notation serves as an optional

skeletal guideline to refer to when listening to and learning the songs.

Marilyn Help sings each song with a starting pitch that is comfortable for her singing voice and that sounds pleasing with her drum. Beyond that, there is no conscious effort on her part as to in what "key" she sings her songs. However, because the connection between what one hears and what one sees is a powerful aural and visual association, the use of key signatures (which first appear in parentheses in the musical manuscript) is an integral part of the skeletal transcription of the songs. In addition, we intentionally omit meter signatures because their placement in the music is so open to interpretation and therefore presents an unnecessarily complex visual interpretation of the music. Nonetheless, we observe that listening to the meter and metrical changes adds an intriguing and compelling aural complexity to the music. Therefore, even though meter signatures are not written in the musical manuscript, references to meter and metrical changes are noted in the text as part of the aural listening experience. Broken bar lines and commas illustrate the phrases in the music, translatable and vocable word groupings, and patterns of recurring vocable formulae. The only exceptions to the use of a skeletal format for the musical transcription is the song "Spot," which features a traditional European American melody, and "Go, My Son," a song written by Native American musicians in Western musical notation.

Interlinear Translation

Jóó	(as you know)
ashí	(two people walking)
lá	(freely, really, discovers)
T'óó	(just)
ga'	(really)
nizhónígo	(beautifully)
baa	(concerning)
hózhǫ	(happiness, harmony)
lá	(freely, really, discovers)
łį́į́	(horse)
ga'	(really)
Ndáá'	(Enemyway)
gi	(at)
béézh	(by means)
ní' áázh	(they, too, arrived)
lá	(freely, really, discovers)

Translation

Jóó ashílá,	Traveling together,
T'óóga' nizhónígo baa hózhǫ lá.	Happy about beauty.
T'óóga' nizhónígo łį́į́ ga'	It is beautiful that they both came on a horse at
Ndáá' gi béézh ní'áázh lá.	the Enemyway ceremony

Note: For pronunciation guidelines, see Appendix A, "The Navajo Language," at the back of the book.

Jóó Ashílá
(Traveling Together)

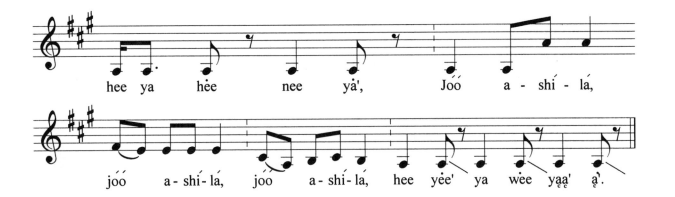

Chapter 2

Roads of Beauty and Happiness

The Song . . .

"Ada'ííztiin, Adahózhǫ́ǫ́"
(Roads of Beauty and Happiness)

"Drive in beauty" is a road sign that frequently appears to travelers fortunate enough to journey through the Navajo Nation. It is a perfect description for the land of the Navajo. The physical landscape radiates with lush hues of reds, pinks, purples, and blues. Indeed, every color of the rainbow may be viewed at one time or another, especially during a sunrise or sunset or an electrifying thunderstorm. Spectacular buttes, mesas, plateaus, arroyos, and rock formations outline the horizon. Each bend in the road reveals diverse housing that includes hogans, traditional Navajo dwellings that today are used mainly for ceremonies. In addition, the Diné live in trailers, cinder block and ranch-style homes, and modest tract houses. The astute observer will note that with rare exceptions, the door of each dwelling faces east, to honor a Navajo tradition that pays respect to the rising sun for its strength and blessings. Since much of the Navajo Nation is in the desert, outhouses may also be found discreetly placed near homes in areas where there is no water supply. And in the far outlying areas of the reservation, some houses have no electricity because of the prohibitive cost of electrical lines.

The Navajo Nation also has verdant ponderosa pine forests, extravagant wildflowers, and deep blue lakes. It is not unusual to see sheep along the roadside as well as

The Navajo Nation Today

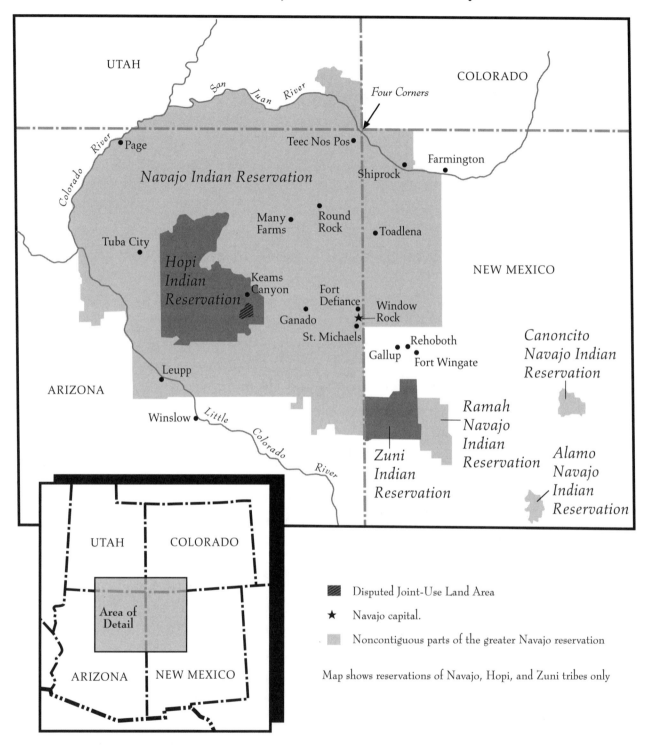

Map 1 The Navajo Nation Today, by Gary Tong.

dogs, horses, and cows. And of course, the viewer may also see the Diné, the People, dressed in contemporary clothing or traditional styles. Women may wear calico broom skirts, velour shirts, and turquoise jewelry with their hair tied in a knot with white yarn. Men may don jeans, a western-style shirt, cowboy boots and hat, and silver belts for their attire. Modern cultural icons are also present, such as pickup trucks, satellite dishes, basketball hoops, and occasional graffiti.

The Navajo Nation is situated on 24,000 square miles of land in the southwestern part of the United States that includes parts of Utah, Arizona, and New Mexico. The Diné were very fortunate: after their incarceration in Fort Sumner from 1864 to 1868, they were allowed to return to a part of their traditional homeland between the four sacred mountains, Sierra Blanca Peak (Dawn or White Shell Mountain) on the east, Mount Taylor (Blue Bead or Turquoise Mountain) on the south, San Francisco Peaks (Abalone Shell Mountain or Yellow Mountain) on the west, and La Plata Mountain (Obsidian Mountain or Black Mountain) on the north. (see Map 1)

Although the Navajo Nation has the largest Indian reservation in the United States, it has the second-largest tribal population. According to the 1999 U.S. Bureau of the Census, the Cherokee Nation has a population of 308,132 and the Navajo Nation, 219,198. Not all Navajos live on their homeland. Because of employment opportunities elsewhere or personal choice, many Navajos have moved away from the four sacred mountains. The Navajo economy depends to a small extent on farming and raising sheep and other livestock and to a large extent on coal, uranium, oil, and natural gas mining and timber harvesting. In addition, crafts such as silversmithing and weaving are significant contributors to Navajo income.

Archeologists and linguists believe that the Navajo, as well as the Apache, are part of the Athabaskan language group that lived in northwestern Canada and Alaska approximately two thousand years ago, after migrating there from Asia. There is no firm agreement as to when the Navajo first arrived in the southwestern part of the United States, nor is there a consensus on which route they took to get there. The Navajo may have migrated to the Southwest anywhere from five hundred to one thousand years ago and may have arrived from the High Plains, the Rocky Mountain chain, or the Great Basin (Brugge 1983, 489). Although scholars can't give a definitive date for the Navajos' arrival in the Southwest, they do agree that the Navajo quickly adapted to selected parts of the Pueblo culture, a group of Native Americans who were already thriving in the area at the time. The Pueblo Indians introduced the Navajo to their effective farming system and to their ceremonies and rituals. When the Spanish arrived in the late sixteenth century, the lifestyle of the Navajo profoundly changed as they were introduced to horses and sheep.

The seventeenth-century Spanish colonists referred to the Navajo as "Apaches de Nabajó," which means "Large Planted

Fields," a name that implies the Navajo were productive farmers. The term *Apaches de Nabajó* may have been derived from one of the Tewa-speaking Pueblos that used the word *Navahu*. According to Kluckhohn and Leighton,

> The view that "Navahu" was a place name used by Tewa-speaking Pueblo Indians and that it might be translated "large area of cultivated lands" has been widely accepted in recent years. This interpretation gains plausibility from the fact that the seventeenth-century Franciscan friar Benavides speaks of the Navajo as "the Apache of the great planted fields." Some scholars claim, however, that the Tewa word really means "to take from the fields." There is also some support for deriving "Navajo" directly from the Spanish in the sense of either a clasp knife or razor or a large, more or less worthless, flat piece of land. (Kluckhohn and Leighton 1974, 24)

Other names for the Navajo were also used at that time. Locke points out that the Navajo, like other tribes during that period, had enemies, all of whom had their own linguistic term for them. He states, "For example, the Hopi called them the Tasavuh which, loosely translated, meant 'head pounders' because of their habit of killing their enemies by pounding them on the head with a stone axe" (Locke 1992, 7). The term *Navajo*, however, has been the most commonly used name to refer to these people

since the seventeenth century. The Navajo call themselves the Diné, a Navajo word that means the People. The spelling of Navajo with a *j* rather than an *h* was officially adopted by the Navajo Nation in 1969.

Although Marilyn acknowledges that scientists, linguists, and historians propose theories about the origin of the Diné and their migration to the Southwest, she does not agree with their conclusions. Rather, she believes in the creation story as told by the Holy People. In fact, Marilyn feels that the Diné have always lived among the four sacred mountains, her beloved homeland. She describes the beauty of her land and environment.

> Where I live is beautiful to me because in the morning when I wake up early, I usually throw my corn pollen or even the white cornmeal to the east before the sun comes up. I always say my prayers in the morning. But before I do that, I step outside, and it is so quiet. Everything is so calm and so still. In the morning when I do not hear hardly anything at all is the time that I feel like I am really close to Mother Earth. And when I go up into the hills, I feel close to Mother Earth because when I look at the plants there, they kind of like wave to me in the breeze. You have this communication with them even though you feel like they are not alive. But they are alive. Even the sky when the clouds move, you know that the clouds are alive, too. And when it begins to rain, I love the smell of the earth. I want to

keep inhaling that wet, nice dirt because when it gets wet, it brings me closer to Mother Earth. I feel that when the sun is just barely coming up, you begin to see the different colors. It seems like it is just so beautiful when you get up and go out there. I am happy to be alive. And that is all.

Our sunrise is orange. There is some orange, yellow, turquoise, and blue. And then it gets lighter and lighter. As you look at the peaks you can see the images of all the different buttes against the hills, the dark shades of the buttes, and then all of a sudden you see the beautiful sunrise on the other side.

You can see the horizon. It is a beautiful color in the morning. The first thing that I always begin to hear is the birds. The birds are always beginning to chirp in the morning.

Our dirt is a really pretty brown color. It is like a dark kind of beige. When you look at the hills and the stones, they have the same color, too. But here and there are darker shades, on certain parts. The dirt itself blends in really well with the surroundings like the grass, rabbitbrush, sage, and other different kinds of plants that we have out there. They all blend in together. (see Plates 4, 5, 6, 7, and 8)

The Song Connection

Marilyn expresses her appreciation for and love of the profound beauty found on the Navajo Nation as she sings the lyrics of the song "Ada'iíztiin, Adahózhǫ́ǫ́," "Roads of Beauty and Happiness."

"Ada'iíztiin, Adahózhǫ́ǫ́"
(Roads of Beauty and Happiness)

Background Information

Our people have sung this song for a very long time. Anybody can sing it. It talks about our homeland, my beautiful homeland. This song came back from Hwééldi, the Long Walk. It kind of ties in with that. There were different songs that originated at that time, when our people were walking back. This one is about remembering

my beautiful homeland. I believe that Kay Bennett sings this same song, too. She heard it from our people and revised it and sang it like that. This is my own personal interpretation of the song.

The words of this song describe the "roads of beauty and happiness" in the Navajo world. The lyrics also express the traditional Navajo blessings of: "Beauty before me. Beauty behind me. Beauty all around me." Although the history of this song is carried only through oral tradition, it may indeed have been composed during the Long Walk period, like the song "Shí Naashá" (see chapter 5).

Information about the music

"Roads of Beauty and Happiness" has both vocables and translatable words in the text. With the exception of the last three vocables in the introduction, the vocable pattern is unique compared to that of the other songs in this book. The vocables are, *"Oo wee yaa na, oo wee yaa na, oo wee yaa na, yaa naa wee na, hee nee ya'."* In addition to the introduction, the vocable pattern occurs during each interlude section and the ending.

The meter of the song switches from a feeling of 6/8 time to 9/8. As is common with these time signatures, there is an underlying feeling of the beat subdivided into sets of three. The drum accompaniment provides a steady beat throughout the song. Although there are many passing notes in the melody, the outline of the tonic, or home triad is continuous. Perhaps the melodic contour of the phrases aurally depicts the highs, lows, and curves of the roads of beauty and happiness on the Navajo Nation.

Because of the sense of an underlying movement in sets of threes and the use of the vocable pattern *"hee nee ya'"* in this song, it meets McAllester's criteria as a tune in the style of a Circle Dance (instructions for the Circle Dance are found in chapter 5). However, Marilyn says that the Diné sing "Roads of Beauty and Happiness" because of the beauty of its melody and the meaning of its words.

Experiencing the music

The easiest way to learn this song is to master the vocable pattern that occurs throughout the song, *"Oo wee yaa na, oo wee yaa na, oo wee yaa na, yaa naa wee na, hee nee ya'."* Once this is accomplished, practice and add one new phrase of Navajo words at a time. Although the musical notation and Navajo words are given for this song, the authors encourage listeners to immerse themselves in the experience of "oral tradition," listening and practicing repeatedly to learn the song in the customary Diné way.

Interlinear Translation

Ada'	(wherever, many)
ííztiin	(roads or paths)
ada	(wherever, many)
hózhǫ́ǫ́	(beauty)
Shí	(I or me)
lą́ą́jí	(front)
hózhǫ́ǫ́	(beauty)
Shí	(I or me)
kéé	(behind)
déé̗	(from)
hózhǫ́ǫ́	(beauty)
Shí	(I or me)
náá	(around)
déé	(from)
hózhǫ́ǫ́	(beauty)

Translation

Ada'ííztiin, adahózhǫ́ǫ́.	Many paths all around, beauty all around.
Shílą́ą́jí hózhǫ́ǫ́.	Beauty before me.
Shíkéédéé̗ hózhǫ́ǫ́.	Beauty behind me.
Shínáádéé hózhǫ́ǫ́.	Beauty all around me.

Ada'ííztiin, Adahózhǫ́ǫ́
(Roads of Beauty and Happiness)

yaa naa wee na, hee nee ya', Oo wee yaa na,

oo wee yaa na, oo wee yaa na, yaa naa wee na, hee nee ya'.

Chapter 3

THE NAVAJO CREATION STORY

The Song . . .

"Shikéyah Nízhónée Bínáashniih"
(Remembering My Beautiful Land)

The last chapter gave the bilagáana and scientific explanation of the appearance of the Navajo in the Southwest hundreds of years ago. Many Navajos, however, discount that version; instead, they wholeheartedly believe in their creation story. In fact, it is just as special to them and their identity as the book of Genesis in the Bible is to Christians. Their creation story is the foundation for their healing ceremonies and indeed for their entire way of life. Their evolution tale reveals the whole spectrum of their beliefs, from the physical geography of their environment to their daily behavior as dictated by the Holy People. Their creation story is a vivid testimonial to the significance of the four sacred

mountains and the Diné need to live between them. During the emergence of the Navajo, the Holy People, deities that are a fundamental part of Navajo culture, gave instructions to the Diné about how to live and act in this, the Glittering World.

Since the creation story was transmitted for hundreds of years by oral tradition, from one generation to the next, many variants in the legend exist, particularly in regard to the number of worlds, the color of each world, and the exact sequence of events that occurred in each. Nonetheless, there is a consensus in creation stories about the primary figures and major occurrences. Because of the sacredness of the story, only a brief outline of the creation myth is given here. Many of the creation stories are told only during the winter season, as dictated by the Holy People. The sources for this paraphrased version are *Navajo History*, edited by Ethelou Yazzie; *Navajo Indian Myths*, by Aileen O'Bryan; and *The Navajo*, by Raymond Locke.

Insect Beings such as Spider Ants, Black Ants, Wasp People, Beetles, Bat People, Dragon Flies, Spider Man and Spider Woman inhabited The First World, also known as the Black World. In addition, there was First Man and First Woman. The Holy People and other spirits lived there, too. Unfortunately, the Beings did not get along very well together. In the hopes of finding a more peaceful place to live, they traveled upward through an opening in the eastern part of their world to the Second World, or Blue World. When the Beings journeyed above to the next world, they took their objectionable and offensive behaviors with them.

The Beings discovered birds and different species of insects, such as locusts and crickets, in the Second World. Wolves, badgers, mountain lions, and wildcats were living there, too. Even Coyote resided in the Blue World. Sadly, the Second World was also a place where there was much suffering. Therefore, when the Beings found another opening in the East, they all traveled to the Third World, or Yellow World.

The physical landscape of historical and sacred land markings began to emerge in the Third World, or Yellow World; the four sacred mountains were formed. In the East was Dawn or White Shell Mountain, in the South was Blue Bead or Turquoise Mountain, in the West was Abalone Shell Mountain, and in the North was Obsidian Mountain. The Third World also had the Center (Soft Goods or Banded Rock Mountain) and the East of Center (Precious Stones or Gobernador Knob). In addition, some of the Holy People had special homes. Turquoise Boy lived in the East, and White Shell Woman resided in the West. There were also mice, chipmunks, squirrels, deer, foxes, and turkeys, as well as spider people, snakes, cat people, and lizards.

Unfortunately, an event occurred in this world that caused its inhabitants much trouble. One day Coyote was playing by the water with a white shell that he had begged for and received from First Man. As he was amusing himself with his antics at the whirlpool, he discovered the child of Water Monster. Coyote quickly grabbed the child and hid it. In retaliation for this act, Water Monster created a great flood. Because First Man was warned about this event, he made preparations for the pending catastrophe. He went to each of the six sacred land sites, taking dirt from each one of them. Then he planted different kinds of foliage with the intent that they would grow tall enough to supply a means for all of the Beings to climb to safety into the next world. After three failed attempts, a female reed grew tall enough for them to exit the Third World and enter safely into the Fourth World, or Glittering World. After the Beings discovered that Coyote had taken Water Monster's baby, he was forced to return it. The turkey was the last animal out of the Third World, narrowly escaping the raging floodwaters. Because he accidentally brushed his tail against the waves, getting it wet, the turkey to this day has white tail feathers.

The monsters who lived in the Glittering World decreed that the Beings would not be allowed to enter their world unless the first creature who appeared passed several tests. Fortunately, the locust arrived first and passed each challenge perfectly, thereby permitting everyone access to the Fourth World.

After they entered the Glittering World, First Man and First Woman recreated the four sacred mountains from the soil that was taken from the Third World. Each site was blessed with the residency of one of the Holy People: White Bead Boy lived in the East Mountain, Turquoise Girl in the South, Abalone Shell Boy in the West, and Obsidian Girl in the North. Other significant events occurred during this period. The Holy People made the first fire and fire poker, sweat bath, and hogan and gave exact instructions on

how to replicate them. And with the assistance of Coyote, the Holy People created and placed the sun, moon, and stars. Critical issues about death, the length of day and night, and the sequence of the seasons were determined. During this time the first known case of adultery occurred, which resulted in the separation of the sexes. Because the Holy People agreed that this division of men and women was unhealthy, they were reunited.

One day First Man and First Woman heard a baby crying on Huerfano Mountain. According to this version of the creation story, "She was born of darkness and the dawn was her father" (Yazzie 1971, 31). The baby girl was called Changing Woman, the most revered and beloved deity of all of the Holy People. Because Changing Woman had the first Kinaaldá, a traditional blessing ceremony that marks a woman's puberty, all women may give birth to children. Soon after her Kinaaldá, Changing Woman was visited by Sun, from which she gave birth to twins, Monster Slayer and Child Born of Water. When her sons grew up, they destroyed the monsters that were plaguing the inhabitants of the Glittering World. Soon after, Changing Woman created the first four Navajo clans from the skin of her body.

The twins had many adventurous escapades as they searched for the identity and home of their father, the Sun. With the assistance of Spider

Woman, they conquered each adversary until they reached him. They hoped that the Sun would help them slay the monsters that were creating havoc throughout their land. The Sun required Monster Slayer and Child Born of Water to pass a series of tests to prove that they really were his sons. Once they accomplished this, the Sun gave them powerful weapons to use to kill the monsters. They destroyed the monsters, including One Walking Giant, He Who Kicked People Off the Cliff, Horned Monster, and Monster Bird. All of the monsters were killed except those of old age, poverty, sleep, lice, and hunger. These monsters were allowed to live in order to remind people to enjoy a long and fruitful life and to celebrate each birth, to appreciate their property, to replenish their bodies with sleep, to stay clean and healthy, and to reap bountiful harvests.

Because the creation story is the anchor and cornerstone for traditional Navajo life, parts of the story are often used as the text for the chants performed in the powerful healing and cleansing ceremonials. The story emphasizes, examines, and explains the need for hózhǫ, or balance, harmony, peace, and beauty. It explores the elements of both good and evil and acknowledges that with the exception of Changing Woman, even the Holy People may exhibit both behaviors. Wyman states, "The Navajo name for supernatural beings, the Holy People *(Diyin Dine'é)*, does not imply that they are virtuously holy but that they are powerful and therefore dangerous. It is man's responsibility to maintain harmonious relations between himself and the Holy People, or at least to avoid them, lest he become injured or ill from their power" (Wyman 1983, 539). Thus the creation story is the genesis for the Diné's well-being. (See Plates 9 and 10)

Marilyn fervently believes in the creation story and shares each part of it with her children.

My children know all about Monster Slayer, Child Born of Water, Changing Woman, First Man, and First Woman. They are part of the Navajo traditional way. If I don't share these stories with my children, these figures will disappear. Because they are so precious to me, I will not let that happen. The creation story offers a great deal of meaning to me because it teaches me values, values that my grandmother and father have taught me, too. My grandmother told me a long time ago about what happened to Monster Slayer, Child Born of Water, and White Shell Woman.

When I was little, I used to change worlds frequently, from that of my grandmother's traditional way, where I was told the Navajo creation story, to that of my mother's contemporary one, where I heard the biblical version. Although my mother took me to church often, I still respected and longed for my

Navajo roots and the Holy People. I wanted to dress up in my traditional Navajo clothes, wear a Navajo knot in my hair, and live the traditional Navajo way each day.

When I think of the creation story, I remember Changing Woman. She is my favorite of all the Holy People. She is also called White Shell Woman. After her puberty ceremony, her Kinaaldá, she was dressed with shell and received her other name. But my boys like Monster Slayer and Child Born of Water best.

The Navajo creation story teaches you discipline; its teachings explain how you should live your life. For example, one tale talks about Coyote, the bad and sneaky one, who stole the baby from its mother, the Water Monster. Its message to us is to behave correctly. It teaches us values and what to do or what not to do. If your children behave like Coyote, then your whole family will be put at risk and you will all suffer the consequences. That is what happened when the great flood came. The creation story teaches self-respect, self-awareness, self-identity, and who you are.

We believe that the Holy People created the earth. They occasionally appear to us, too. Last summer I heard a story about an old lady who lived out toward Rocky Ridge, Arizona. Her daughter thought that she was going out of her mind because she kept saying, "Somebody's going to visit us today," over and over again. It was driving her daughter nuts. Pretty soon the daughter said, "Don't say that anymore! I think you're crazy!" But later on in the afternoon, around twelve or one o'clock, the daughter heard what sounded like a big jet landing in a big wind. She went out to investigate and was shocked to see two persons standing there. As soon as she looked at their image one of them put up his hand and her head immediately dropped down. She couldn't look back up. One of them started talking to her in Navajo and told her, "Grandchild, we've been trying to come and see you for the past two days, but you were not at home. But today you are here, and we want you to tell the Diné, the People, that they must remember the traditional ways and go back, back to the waters in the different places. That is why you are having a drought. The elderly people are not being respected. You have to tell the people that they have to take their turquoise back to the water so that they can have more rain. Otherwise bad things are going to happen. You must warn the people." One of them was dressed all in white, and one was dressed all in turquoise. They were the Holy People from the East and the South. They came to give us their message about the drought.

The Song Connection

Creation story songs are not included in this chapter because of the sacredness of their text and music and their ceremonial function. Instead Marilyn sings a song that describes the beauty of her native land, situated within the four sacred mountains, landmarks that are beloved gifts from the Holy People and powerful daily reminders of the creation story.

"Shikéyah Nízhónée Bínáashniih"
(Remembering My Beautiful Land)

Background Information

"Remembering My Beautiful Land" is a social song, and everybody sings it. It talks about remembering the land that you are from. And it probably refers to the Long Walk because that is when our people were in that place that they call Fort Sumner. Our people made up songs when they were there just like I make up songs now. I learned this song on my own from my friend Elva Benson. She is the one who passed away a long time ago. I thought a lot of the songs that she sang were so neat. She was singing this song one day and I thought, "I want to sing the same songs that she sings," and so that is what I did. She passed away fifteen years ago or something like that.

I have known this song a long time. My own children know it, but I have not yet taught it to my students at school. This song is really a special one. You can do a dance to it, too.

This song is an old, old one. People, certain ones, have just kept singing it and singing it. It is old.

A common theme in Marilyn's tradi-tional songs is the focus on the beauty of the land, the Navajo Nation that lies among the four sacred mountains. Marilyn suggests that many Diné know this music. As is the case with many traditional Navajo songs that are transmitted orally, the exact origin of this music is unknown.

Information about the music

"Remembering My Beautiful Land" is a song that shares many of the same musical characteristics as "Roads of Beauty and Happiness" (chapter 2) and "The Long Walk" (chapter 5). All three have an under-lying feeling of the beat subdivided into sets of three, as well as triple meter. In addition, each includes the vocable pattern *"hee nee ya'."* Since the rhythm and vocables meet McAllester's criteria for Circle Dance songs, each of these falls into that style of music (McAllester 1992, 37). However, Marilyn performs a Two-step, or "high-stepping" dance to this song rather than a Circle Dance.

There are three vocable patterns in this song. The first formula, *"hee yee' yą́ą́ ą́',"* only occurs at the beginning to introduce the tune. Then an extensive second vocable pattern follows that appears throughout the piece, *"Ei nee ya hoo' ho, hee nee ya', Ei nee ya hoo' oo' a hoo ghąą' ąą, Ei nee ya hoo' a hoo', hee nee ya'."* The third vocable formula is used as an independent phrase, *"hee nee ya',"* as well as part of the extensive second vocable pattern.

The melody starts on the tonic, or home tone with the first vocable pattern and then leaps an octave higher. Although many passing tones embellish the tune, the basic outline of the tonic chord occurs throughout, a typical Navajo music characteristic (McAllester and Mitchell 1983, 606).

Experiencing the music

The three vocable patterns in "Remembering My Beautiful Land" can be identified when they occur in the song. Focus on one pattern at a time and practice singing them with the recording. Once the vocable formulas are learned, add the other Navajo words.

Marilyn dances the Two-step, or high-stepping foot movement with this song. Once partners are selected, female's choice, the dancers move in a clockwise direction around the circle with the male partner on the outside. The feet step in a sprightly manner to the beat. Either foot may begin first as long as the partners are in unison.

Interlinear Translation

Shi	(My)
kéyah	(land, under my feet)
nízhónée	(very beautiful)
bí	(it)
náash	(again I)
niih	(remember)
K'ad	(now)
niki	(start)
deesháál	(I will go)
nisin	(I think)
k'ad	(now)
nikini	(I am going)

Translation

Shikéyah nízhónée bínáashniih.　　　I remember my beautiful land.
K'ad nikideeshááł, nisin, k'ad nikini.　　I want to go home now, I am going home now.

Shikéyah Nízhónée Bínáashniih
(Remembering My Beautiful Land)

drum

Hee yee' yąą' ą', Ei nee ya hoo' ho, hee nee ya',

ei nee ya hoo' oo' a hoo ghąą' ąą, ei nee ya hoo a hoo', hee nee ya',

Ei nee ya hoo' ho, hee nee ya', ei nee ya hoo' oo' a hoo' ghąą' ąą,

ei nee ya hoo' a hoo', hee nee ya',

Shi - ké - yah ní - zhó - née bí - náash - niih,

Shi-ké-yah ní-zhó-née bí-náash-niih, K' - ad ni-ki-dee-shaał ni-sin, K' -

ad ni - ki - ni ya hoo' a hoo', hee nee ya',

Ei nee ya hoo' ho', hee nee ya',

ei nee ya hoo' oo' a hoo ghąą' ąą,

ei nee ya hoo' a hoo', hee nee ya'.

Chapter 4

Hózhǫ –
Beauty in Navajo Ceremonies and Culture

The Song . . .

"Ii hii yee, Ii hii yee"
(Feather Dance Song)

If you were to select one word that effectively and powerfully describes the spirit or heart of an entire culture, what would it be? Is there an inclusive term that encompasses the myriad of cultural components, such as languages, laws, traditions, celebrations, and religions? For example, what word would describe the spirit or heart of the United States of America? Would *freedom* be an accurate noun, or would *democracy* be better? The Diné have such an inclusive word; it captures the heart of their culture and permeates all aspects of their life. It is the central hub from which all other spikes stem. Their word is *hózhǫ*, the cornerstone and foundation of Navajo life and values.

There are numerous synonyms for hózhǫ: *goodness, harmony, balance, beauty, happiness, orderliness, blessedness, pleasantness, perfection, success,* and *well-being* (Wyman 1983, 537; McAllester 1992, 44; Iverson 1990, 32). Marilyn Help defines it simply: "Hózhǫ is beauty, walking in beauty. It is a really good feeling within yourself and your mind."

But hózhǫ is more than just a word; it is an all-encompassing philosophy that supplies the underlying framework for the Diné value system and way of life. In fact, because it is so influential in Navajo culture, outsiders refer to hózhǫ as the basis of the Navajo religion, even though Navajos do not call it that. Since living in hózhǫ́ is so holistic, there is no need for the separate word *religion* in the Navajo language (Kluckhohn and Leighton 1974, 44). Locke supports this idea: "The Navajo's concept of religion is so total that it can be said that there is no such thing as religion in Navajo culture because everything is religious. Everything a Navajo knows—his shelter, his fields, his livestock, the sky above him and the ground upon which he walks—is holy" (Locke 1992, 5). McAllester further supports this idea:

> They see the power of animals, birds, and insects, and also of earth, water, wind, and sky, not just in a sentimental way but as active potencies that have a direct influence on human life. All of these forces may speak directly to human beings and may teach them the songs, prayers and ritual acts that make up the ceremonials. At the center of this relationship with the natural world is the concept of *hózhǫ́* (beauty, blessedness, harmony) which must be maintained, and which, if lost, can be restored by means of ritual. The prayers invoke this state over and over at their conclusions. (McAllester 1992, 44)

Indeed, the Diné strive to live in harmony with Mother Earth, the sun, the moon, and the stars, as well as with animals, material things, each other, and the Holy People.

The concept of hózhǫ́ is very much alive in traditional and contemporary Navajo culture. Marilyn Help exemplifies this when she teaches her children the Diné way. She wants them to see their world from an inclusive viewpoint, to live in hózhǫ́, and to honor and respect the Holy People and their teachings. Marilyn discusses and defines *hózhǫ́ǫ́jí*, which is also the name of the ceremonial that Frank Mitchell, a Navajo medicine man, describes as "the backbone of the Navajo Nation."

> *Hózhǫ́ǫ́jí* is the way you live on a daily basis. It is how you present yourself to others, what we call *k'e*. K'e is how I raise my children. If I talk to my children, I do not use the devil words. When I say something to my child, I say, "'*áashinee' shiyázhí*," which means from the bottom of my heart I love that person. I always use that word for my child, *shiyázhí*. That has a holistic meaning for me because in my world I combine everything together; that is *hózhǫ́ǫ́jí*. Hózhǫ́ǫ́jí is anything in life that is good. It is *iiná*, which means life itself is good, the good side and the good way. This is what I believe. I believe in living life to its fullest, but in a good way. To me this is what *hózhǫ́ǫ́jí* means.

> Nature and Mother Earth are really important to us, and the reason is because she gives gifts to us all of the time, our water, our food, and our plants. She provides us with everything, even the wood for the chairs that we sit in and the metal for the vehicles that we drive. My grandmother told me about my

connection with Mother Earth when I was a little girl. She told me to listen to the plants, the sky, and the clouds. She told me that my mouth was very holy because if you say something harsh to somebody, it could have a disastrous consequence. The Holy People made it that way. Be careful of what you say because the Holy People are listening all of the time. They will hear you.

Mother Earth, female, and Father Sky, male, are very special to us; they face each other. There are males and females in all parts of our world, including the stars, animals, flowers, and trees. My grandmother told me to go out and pray to my surroundings and my world with an intent and sincere heart. If I do that, I will know that the Holy People are there and have heard me. I will walk in beauty.

The Diné make continuous efforts to live their lives in hózhǫ́. But events and accidents can occur that lead to disharmony and imbalance.

Like many other cultures in the world, the Diné accept the fact that both good and evil exist. Wyman describes this Navajo belief: "Being all-inclusive, the universe contains evil as well as good, not as abstract ethical concepts, but as complementary components of it—the controlled, harmonious, orderly, and the uncontrolled, inharmonious, disorderly portions of every unit or complex in it" (Wyman 1983, 536). Hence the evils of the world may overcome the good forces that cause imbalance. Locke describes some of these evils: "Disease, misfortune, distress and other evils caused by failure to observe taboos and ceremonial regulations, by spirits, by natural elements or phenomena such as whirlwinds, lightning, water or, worst of all, witchcraft, are reasons for a ceremonial (Locke 1992, 48)." Wyman describes "improper contact" that may cause imbalance:

Improper contact may occur while hunting, trapping, killing, eating, mishandling, or being injured by an animal, using things it has been in contact with, such as firewood, stones, and the like; burning cactus for firewood, especially for cooking, being struck by whirlwinds or by lightning, or seeing or eating animals killed by it, or having anything to do with objects affected by it; mistakes or neglect in ceremonial procedure, or transgressions of ceremonial restrictions; improper burial of the dead, using their possessions, or any sort of contact with them or their belongings; or even dreaming of any of these things. (Wyman 1983, 544)

In addition, Kluckhohn and Leighton list traditional taboos that may trigger disharmony:

Avoid trees struck by lightning.
Never kill coyotes, bears, snakes, and selected birds.
Never eat fish, waterbirds, water animals.
Never eat raw meat.

Do not use the point of a knife to cut a melon.

Do not comb your hair at night.

Never step over another person when sleeping in a hogan at night. (Kluckhohn and Leighton 1974, 201)

Even though events inevitably occur that can cause disharmony, the Diné can take precautions to prevent imbalance. For instance, Marilyn and her father say daily morning prayers to the Holy People to invoke their good will and to prevent misfortune.

My dad always used to tell us to get up early in the morning and run outside to the east and greet the Holy People. He said, "Get up early and face all of those things that will be coming to you, all the hardship and all of the troubles that you will be faced with in the future. If you get up early and run, you will have a strong heart for all of those things." When I was a little girl, I used to think, "Oh, I hate running. I don't want to run. Why can't I just sleep?" We used to get up at five or six o'clock, just barely when you can see the dawn, and that's when we'd be running. I can remember the feel of the cold wind and the breezes blowing my hair back. And I'd be running and running after my sister. Sometimes we would cheat. We'd sit right there in the middle of the path, and then when all the other children would be coming back, we'd turn around and start running again. But now, when my dad says "jump" in the morning, I don't say how high; I'm out of bed and out the door by the time he finishes his sentence. And do you know what, I say the same thing to my children, "Get up and go run!" Sometimes they do it and sometimes they don't.

I go outside and pray to the Holy People early in the morning. They say that if you sleep in and stay in bed, the Holy People will say, "Well, I guess this person is already too rich. I guess he doesn't want anything in his life, so we'll just bypass him." And then they will ignore you and won't give you your blessing because you chose to sleep in.

Marilyn and her family also have mountain smokes in the morning to ensure good thoughts and safety.

We have the mountain smoke to keep our minds clear and to give us clean thoughts. There are many bad energies in the world that can come to you without your knowing it. If you have a mountain smoke in the morning, it will clear your mind. For example, if someone is trying to do something to you in a "Navajo way" that is not good, the mountain smoke will protect you. In addition, you should wear turquoise every day for protection.

The mountain smoke comes from herbs and plants that the medicine men gather and dry. You crush up the herbs, like tobacco, roll it in corn husks, and then smoke it. However, before the medicine men gather the herbs, they must give Mother Earth a gift, like turquoise or something. They tell us that if you give Mother Earth a present before you take something from her, what you take will be more meaningful to you because you have made a connection with her. You are giving something back instead of just taking something and owning it for yourself.

Even though the Diné take preventive measures to maintain hózhǫ́, such as greeting the Holy People at dawn with prayers or having a mountain smoke, events may still create disharmony. If a misfortune should happen, a Navajo may be a patient in a curative ceremonial designed to restore hózhǫ́. A specific sequence of events usually occurs before the ceremonial performance.

The patient, "the one sung over," usually consults a diviner, a visionary who has the gift to analyze a problem through stargazing, hand trembling, or listening. Once the diviner diagnoses what caused the malady, he or she recommends the appropriate ceremony for the cure. Locke describes a diviner's power: "A diviner interprets the involuntary motions of his hand, or the thing he sees or hears while in a trancelike state, and discovers the cause of the trouble. He determines the proper ritual for a cure and may recommend a singer (Locke 1992, 48). In addition to this function, a diviner may have a vision to locate water in the desert, find missing objects, or identify an adulterer or adulteress (Kluckhohn and Leighton 1974, 210). After a diagnosis, plans

for the ceremony, such as hiring a medicine person and setting the date, begin.

A medicine person, male or female, conducts the ceremony. Navajos refer to their healer as "the singer." The medicine person must have an excellent memory because each ceremony consists of numerous ritual acts, which include hundreds of lines of poetry in prayers and songs and must all be learned by heart and performed perfectly. Therefore it is usual for a medicine person to specialize in and perform only two or three ceremonies. If the medicine person makes a mistake in the ritual, the Holy People may decide not to give their blessings and the ceremony will fail to restore hózhǫ́ to the patient, "the one sung over." In addition to praying and singing, the medicine person acts as a master of ceremonies who directs his assistants and patient in the ritual. A "singer" negotiates his fee with the family of "the one sung over," and it is based on several factors. Kluckhohn and Leighton state, "The fee varies with his reputation, the rarity of the ceremonial knowledge involved, the time spent and the distance traveled for the ceremony, and the degree of his relationship to the patient" (Kluckhohn and Leighton 1974, 226). Unfortunately, the cost of a ceremony may dictate whether or not the patient will go through with the healing ritual.

Some ceremonies require sandpaintings or drypaintings. These pictures, which the singer and his assistants create from colorful sands, pollen, stones, and other materials, re-create designs prescribed by the Holy People. The medicine person gives his assistants directions for this elaborate production.

Because the Diné value the sacredness of their sandpaintings, they destroy them after each ceremony. According to Locke, the Navajo have anywhere from six hundred to one thousand different ceremonial sandpaintings in their ceremonial repertoire (Locke 1992, 50). Wyman elaborately describes their use and function:

> This is a symbolic picture, often large and complicated, of the protagonist of the myth that sanctions and explains the ceremonial or the Holy People he encounters in his mythical adventures, accompanied by many subsidiary symbols. It is made on the floor of the hogan by trickling dry pigments from between the thumb and flexed forefinger on a background of the tan-colored sand smoothed out with a weaving batten. The pigments are red, yellow, and white sandstone, charcoal pulverized on a grinding stone, and a few mixtures—charcoal and white sand for a bluish color, red and black for brown, and red and white for pink. Any man who knows how may work on them under the direction of the singer, who seldom takes part except to lay down some fundamental lines. Women do not take part or even watch for fear of injury from the powers invoked, although a woman past child-bearing age may grind the pigments. When the Holy People taught the protagonists of the myths how to reproduce their sacred pictures, which they kept rolled up on clouds, they forbade their reproduction in permanent form lest they be soiled or damaged, so the designs that are rigidly prescribed are transmitted in memory from singer to apprentice. A sandpainting may be a foot or less in diameter or one around 20 feet across made in a special large hogan. The average painting in a family hogan is about six feet in diameter. Depending on its complexity it may be completed by from four to six men in three to five hours. (Wyman 1983, 551)

Although one can buy sandpaintings in souvenir shops on the reservation, the artists modify each picture to honor its sacredness.

The medicine person learns the ceremony through apprenticeship. He or she acts as an assistant to an experienced teacher and masters the rituals of the ceremony through repetition and practice. The apprentice pays the medicine person for the training. In addition to acquiring the songs and prayers for a ceremony, the medicine person must also have a sacred medicine bundle containing holy artifacts used for healing. Wyman gives a detailed description of items that may be included in a medicine bundle:

> Among these are gourd, rawhide, or deer or bison hoof rattles; a bull-roarer, a flat stick pointed at one end, with a buckskin thong attached to the other, which is whirled to make a sound like thunder and thus intimidate evil; medicine stoppers, small feathered wands

used to protect, stir, taste, sprinkle, and apply medicines; smooth canes or digging sticks, to remove medicines from sacks; talking prayer sticks of wood or stone; tie-ons (chant tokens, head feather bundles), little bundles of fluffy eagle plumes one of which is tied to the patient's forelock on the last day of a chant to facilitate recognition by supernaturals and humans; a brush of eagle quill feathers used for asperging, protecting medicines, and exorcising evil; a fur collar, a badge of recognition for singer or patient (Shootingway requires one of otter or beaver skin), with an attached eagle wing bone whistle to signal, summon, and attract the Holy People; a fire drill handle, tip, and fireboard (hearth); woolen unraveling strings with eagle plume feathers tied to the ends; medicine cups of abalone or turtle shell; prehistoric arrowheads, spearpoints, knives, drills, and the like, which have exorcistic properties and are used to cut ceremonial materials (flints); a stone club, Monster Slayer's weapon; materials for jewel (bits of turquoise, abalone and white shell, and jet), reed (cigarette), and cut wooden prayer stick offerings; interesting or oddly shaped stones, concretions, or fossils, and small cylinders or animal figurines made of banded or white aragonite; quartz crystals; and many sacks of paints, cornmeal, pollens, and herbal medicines. (Wyman 1983, 549)

Wyman also notes that there is a dis-

tinction between a medicine bundle and a medicine pouch. The medicine bundle stores numerous artifacts for all ceremonial usage, whereas the medicine pouch holds materials for only one ritual. Because of the sacredness of the medicine person's bundle, the relatives of the singer receive it upon his death or bury it with him or her (Wyman 1983, 548–49).

The singer performs the ceremony in a hogan. The ceremonies vary in length from several hours to nine days. Regardless of their performance time, every ceremony requires the reciting of prayers and singing of songs by the medicine person and his assistants. Wyman states:

> Most important is the singing, usually accompanied by a rattle, led by the singer but joined by all (usually men) who know how. Singing accompanies nearly every act and in Navajo thought it is the one indispensable part of any ceremonial; without it there can be no cure, indeed no chantway. A few songs, if nothing else, may do some good. Knowledge of several hundred songs is required for most chants. Prayers are said at intervals and communal pollen prayer occurs at or near the close of ceremonies. (Wyman 1983, 550)

The creation story, or other traditional myths related to it, are the basis for each ceremony. McAllester states, "These chants are 'classic' in that they have a tradition going back for generations, no one knows how many; they have enormous scope—one chant may contain over five hundred songs and the texts comprise many thousands of lines of religious poetry; they contain in their prayers and songs, and in the related myths, the meaning the Navajos find in the natural and supernatural worlds" (McAllester 1992, 43). Ceremonial songs and prayers are extremely powerful. In fact, they are rarely performed or heard out of context; to do so compromises their sacredness and healing power.

Each part of the ceremony has its own song, as described by McAllester and Mitchell: "The music includes songs for blessing the ceremonial hogan, introducing prayers, performing specific ritual acts such as making offerings to the deities, making ritual fire, bathing, drying and blessing 'the one sung over,' ritual dancing, and making drypaintings, to list a few examples" (McAllester and Mitchell 1983, 607). Memorizing all of the prayers and songs required for a ceremony is daunting. Kluckhohn and Leighton describe it this way: "The singer who knows one nine-day chant must learn at least as much as a man who sets out to memorize the whole of a Wagnerian opera: orchestral score, every vocal part, all the details of the settings, stage business, and each requirement of costume" (Kluckhohn and Leighton 1974, 229). Because of the intense desire on the part of some Diné to carry on their sacred traditions, they give opportunities and encouragement to young Navajos to learn the sacred ceremonies. In fact, Marilyn Help is encouraging her oldest son, Lyle, to learn the Diné way and to pursue his interest in becoming a medicine man.

Traditional Navajo rituals require several different instruments. Made out of a variety of materials, the most common is the rattle. The singer shakes the rattle as an accompaniment to the sacred songs. An overturned basket, struck like a drum with a braided yucca leaf striker, supplies the background beat for some songs. In addition, at certain moments the medicine person may whirl a bull-roarer. Singers play the water drum to accompany songs in the Enemyway, producing a resonant "heartbeat" for the performance of Squaw Dances late into the night.

Although the focus of the ceremony is the patient, "the one sung over," each ritual also involves the entire extended family. Since ceremonies last anywhere from one to nine days, the family may assist in finding the ingredients needed for sandpaintings, buying food for large groups of people, butchering sheep, and cleaning the hogan (Locke 1992, 48). In addition, the family serves and welcomes all of the visitors and guests who attend the ceremony. And sometimes the "one sung over" and his family combine finances to pay the medicine person's fee. In exchange for their help, the extended family reaps benefits. They, too, may share in the prayers and blessings invoked for the patient and the restoration of hózhǫ́. Ceremonies also provide a ready-made forum for social gatherings and interactions with other Navajos who attend the ceremony. Unfortunately, excessive drinking by the guests occasionally distracts from the sacred purpose of the event.

Ceremonies have descriptive names such as Blessingway, Shootingway, Enemyway, Nightway, and Mountainway. Each ceremony has a purpose and function, and some ceremonies have strictures on their performance. For example, performance of the Enemyway is during the summer and of the Nightway in the winter.

Marilyn describes the performance of two healing ceremonies for her, "the one sung over." The first ceremony was the "snake doing" ritual, a ceremony that restores hózhǫ́ after one offends nature by accidentally touching a snakeskin. The ceremony, performed by a medicine man, was held in a hogan and lasted one-half day. He created a sandpainting of snakes as part of the ritual to repair the damage done to her.

She was also "the one sung over" in the Mountainway ceremony. Her father's concern was that some of the Diné might become jealous because of Marilyn's successful career. In fact, he feared that they might even resort to witchcraft to bring harm to her. Therefore her father insisted that she go to a stargazer to analyze the problem and diagnose the appropriate ceremony for the cure. The stargazer said that she needed to have a Mountainway performed and recommended

a medicine person to conduct the ritual. She describes it as follows:

The Mountainway was performed for me and my children to protect us. We were in this very old medicine man's hogan on a cold night. My dad was there, too. It took three or four hours for the medicine man to complete the ceremony. We had a mountain smoke as part of the ritual, and it was really special. Everything was done in the evening so that the stars could provide their energy. This ceremony did not involve a sandpainting, just the chanting of Monster Slayer and selected monsters. The medicine man sang and sang the whole time as he accompanied himself on the rattle.

It is challenging for a cultural outsider, who has never been the "one sung over," to fully comprehend the sacredness and power of a ceremonial and its curative spirit. But because living in hózhǫ́ is a fundamental part of the Diné culture, to understand the Navajo world, an outsider must attempt to respect the values, ideas, and rituals that are such integral components of it.

The Song Connection

Since ceremonial songs are rarely performed out of context in order to preserve their sacredness and healing powers, they are not included in this book. But occasionally a sacred song takes on a new life as a social tune and crosses over to the secular music genre. The "Feather Dance Song" is an excellent example of this type of tune. It originally came from the Fire Dance, a part of the Yeibichai, or Nightway ceremony. Throughout the years, as it was passed on by oral tradition, it emerged as a popular song that is often sung and performed in social contexts. Marilyn shares her version of the "Feather Dance Song."

"Ii hii yee, Ii hii yee"
(Feather Dance Song)

Background Information

I learned this song when I saw some people performing it. They were singing it, and I just picked it up. And ever since then I have remembered it. It is a rhythmic type of song for people to do their dances. My dad did not teach me this one.

I have also seen the dance with it. The dancers just stand there in one place and go back and forth and back and forth. They hold the wedding basket in front of them and then just go back and forth. The sash is not connected with the basket; it is just around your waist. You can dress up with a sash belt. And sometimes they dance with a feather or a gourd. They also hold juniper and move it back and forth.

Although Marilyn has never danced the "Feather Dance Song," she has seen it performed many times. She notes that there are several versions of the dance. One variation is restricted to female dancers, who stand side by side, facing the same direction in a line. They step in place to the beat, alternating between their left and right feet. Each dancer holds the same type of object—a

feather, basket, gourd, or juniper branch—and moves it to the music. Another variant, the "Red Sash Belt Dance Song," is for male and female dancers who perform as partners. The male dancers in the group unwrap their partner's belt, and then all of the dancers perform choreographed designs with the female belts.

Roseann Willink, a University of New Mexico instructor of Navajo, describes the colorful variant of the music that she calls the "Red Sash Belt Dance Song." The Diné have taken the song out of its traditional ceremonial context and adapted it as a social song and dance. Both male and female dancers perform this colorful version of the "Feather Dance Song." Willink shares her insight regarding the Navajo woman's attire, including the significance and meaning of the belt referred to in the song. She says that all jewelry and everything a Navajo woman wears have meaning and significance, including her belt. A Diné woman wears her belt to assist her in making decisions; the belt has a "thinking" value associated with it. When a woman wears her belt to a meeting, it gives her power. That is why Navajo women wear a belt for the girls' puberty rite, Kinaaldá—it gives them strength. A Navajo saying refers to this custom, *"Sís béé dááhólíí . . . ,"* which means, "It's not up to me; it's up to the belts." These words are included in Marilyn's version of the "Feather Dance Song." In fact, all of the other words in the song are vocables.

Marilyn supports the idea that traditional clothing, including the sash belt, marks the Diné so that the Holy People will recognize them.

Well, they say that a long time ago Changing Woman was dressed with all white: white shell beads, white shell earrings, and a white shell bracelet. From the beginning she was called White Shell Woman, so she dressed up in white shells. Even her belt was white and made of white shells. The beads on her moccasins were made out of white shells, too. Because Changing Woman dressed like that, we dress in her image and wear our turquoise and our jewelry. This represents that we are introducing ourselves to the Holy People. They recognize us because of our jewelry and when we say our clan names. Even in the afternoon when they see you wearing your jewelry, they say, "That's my child right there." That is what they say to you.

The Holy People recognize you when you wear your Navajo knot. We need to be wearing these types of things. That is how my grandma was, my grandma on my dad's side. She used to wear her jewelry all of the time, and she told me to do that, too.

She said, "Don't ever just be plain." We have to be wearing some sort of jewelry all of the time. And since she told me that, I have always worn my jewelry. We use our jewelry as a protector, too. It is like an armor against all evil. That is why we wear our jewelry, for that purpose.

Information about the music

The "Feather Dance Song" consists of vocables except for the words *"Sís béé dááhólíí,"* "It's up to the belts." As Marilyn said, the rhythmic patterns of eighth, quarter, and half notes are compelling and beckon the listener to move in response to the music. Although the beat stays steady, the meter switches from fours to sixes, depending on the vocable patterns. The pentatonic melody line differs from the usual focus on the tonic as the magnetic "home base." Instead the melodic notes use all of the notes of the scale except for the fourth and the seventh.

Experiencing the music

As with the other songs in this book, orally is the most traditional way to learn the "Feather Dance Song." After repeated hearings, the vocable patterns are readily identifiable, especially the beginning and ending vocable formulas, *"Ii hii yee, ii hii yee, o-ho-ho-ho"* and *"O-ho wee, o-ho-ho, ii hii yee hee."*

The footwork for this dance is the same, whether a feather, gourd, or juniper branch is used as a prop. Women and girls, standing shoulder to shoulder in a line facing the same direction, traditionally perform this dance. Each woman or girl steps to the beat while alternating the feet in place. The dancers may use any type of feather for their prop when they perform it out of a ceremonial contest, but for rituals the dancers hold an eagle feather. The dancer holds a feather in each hand and moves the feathers back and forth to the beat, alternating the hands as they move "in and out." The cedar branches are held and used the same way.

When the dancers use gourd rattles as props, they are held in front of the chest, one in each hand, and shaken to the beat with the hands and forearms parallel to each other. Because women and girls tradition-

ally perform these dance variants, Marilyn requests that users of this book honor this custom, as well as the time strictures for this dance. Even though the song has a vibrant existence as social music, since this dance is taken from the Yeibichai, or Nightway ceremony, a ritual performed only in the wintertime, she wants this tradition to be followed.

The version of this dance that uses the wedding basket is more complex. It involves a series of stops and starts with the feet and a more complex rhythmic choreography with the baskets, and so it is not included in this text. The Red Sash Belt Dance is also omitted because of its difficulty.

Interlinear Translation

Sís   (belt)
béé   (with)
dáá   (many)
hólíí   (it's up to)

Translation

Sís béé dááhólíí.   "It's up to the belts."

Ii hii yee, Ii hii yee
(Feather Dance Song)

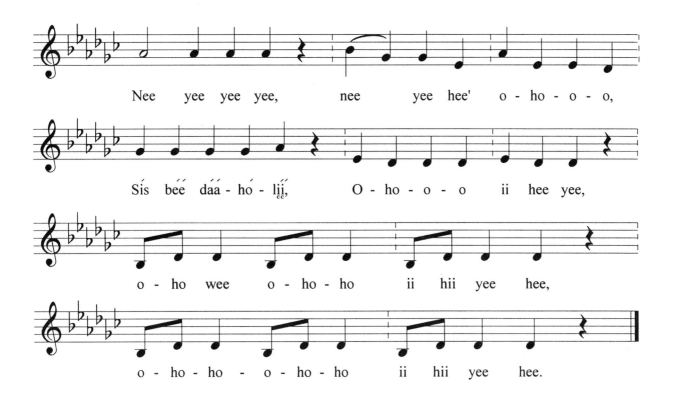

Nee   yee   yee yee,   nee   yee hee' o - ho - o - o,

Sis   beé daá - hó - lįį,   O - ho - o - o   ii   hee yee,

o - ho   wee   o - ho - ho   ii hii   yee   hee,

o - ho - ho - o - ho - ho   ii hii   yee   hee.

Chapter 5

THE LONG WALK

The Song . . .

"Shí Naashá"
(I Am Going)

Generation after generation of the Diné tell stories about a tragic event that occurred to them during the mid-nineteenth century: the Long Walk, the forced journey that led to their incarceration at Fort Sumner, New Mexico, from 1864 to 1868. The events that precipitated this exile started as early as the seventeenth century, when slave and livestock raids were rampant between the Navajo and other Indian tribes as well as the Spaniards. Although raiding was an unwelcome way of life for all of the inhabitants of the Southwest for many years, this annoyance came to a head after the United States won its war with Mexico in 1848 and set its sights on occupying the area for economic gain.

The U.S. government was determined to bring peace to the territory and get all of its occupants, especially the Navajo, under its control.

Unfortunately for the Diné, a series of events took place during their negotiations with the U.S. government that led to their forced internment at Bosque Redondo, an area in southeastern New Mexico that surrounds Fort Sumner. A great influence on the treaties made between the two parties was the inherent cultural makeup of the Navajo. The Navajo had no "one" leader to discuss and decide vital issues that affected the whole tribe. Instead there were many headmen, each in charge of his own clan. It took a long time for the U.S. government to realize that a negotiation with one headman did not guarantee an agreement with all of the Navajo leaders. As agreements were made and then broken, the trust factor between the United States and the Diné was hopelessly compromised.

In addition to the cultural challenge of dealing with numerous Navajo leaders, several encounters between the U.S. government and the Diné ended tragically. On August 31, 1849, U.S. representatives James Calhoun and Colonel John Washington met with selected Navajos in the Chuska Mountains to explain their plans to build forts and settle U.S. citizens in the area. Unfortunately, during the negotiations a dispute arose over the ownership of a horse that led to the killing of seven Navajos, including Narbona, a respected Navajo elder. Although Narbona's murder was viewed as an outrageous act by the Navajo, the government continued with its plans to infiltrate the area. Fort Defiance was built as intended in the 1850s in the heart of Navajo country.

Another tragedy occurred on July 12, 1858. Captain William T. H. Brooks, commander of Fort Defiance, wanted retribution after his black slave, Jim, was killed by a Navajo. He sent his troops on a rampage to find the murderer. One reluctant Navajo headman eventually presented Captain Brooks with the body of a dead Navajo man to make amends. This act only further provoked Brooks because the coroner at the fort proved that the body brought in by the Navajos was not that of the murderer; the real culprit was still at large. This event caused bad feelings to escalate—the Navajo and Americans were heading for a major conflict.

At the end of April 1860, Manuelito and Barboncito, two respected Navajo leaders, led their comrades on an attack of Fort Defiance and were narrowly defeated. This was followed by yet another atrocity. On September 22, 1861, at Fort Fauntleroy an outrageous massacre of Navajo men, women, and children took place over a disputed horse race. The American soldiers were accused of cutting the bridle of a Navajo rider's horse, causing him to lose the race. When the Navajos protested the outcome, complete chaos ensued, which included the random shooting of innocent victims.

Each of these events set the stage for the employment of a more forceful policy toward the Navajo by the U.S. government. Since the treaties they had negotiated with different tribal headmen had little effect on their ultimate goal of controlling Navajo slave and livestock raids on other inhabitants of the territory, a new plan was created and implemented by Brigadier General James Carleton, who in 1862 had been appointed U.S. Army commander in the New Mexico Territory. While many American troops were occupied fighting the American Civil War in the east, Carleton decided to keep his forces fighting and containing the Navajo in the west. His goal was to control both the Apache and the Navajo so that the non-Indians in the area were safe. In addition, Carleton, struck with gold fever, wanted safe, free access to explore the mineral possibilities in the Southwest (Iverson 1990, 41). He planned to remove all of the Apache and Navajo in the Southwest to Fort Sumner, a fort built especially for this purpose in the middle of Bosque Redondo, a round grove of cottonwood trees by the Pecos River. Carleton felt that once the Indians were incarcerated at Fort Sumner, they could be converted and assimilated into American society. Although Carleton was warned that his chosen site in southeastern New Mexico was basically uninhabitable, he was adamant about pursuing his plan.

Carleton enlisted Kit Carson, the famed frontiersman, to assist in his goal of rounding up the Apache and Navajo, forcing them to leave their homelands, and moving them to Fort Sumner. Carson, also known as the "rope thrower" to the Navajo, began his campaign to defeat them in July 1863. He was ordered to give Carleton's message, "Surrender or be killed," to the Diné (Iverson 1990, 42). Carson's strategy was simple and effective: destroy all crops, water wells, and hogans and then chase the Navajo until they surrendered. He chose Canyon de Chelly as the focus of his purge. In early January 1864 Carson planned a rendezvous with Captain A. W. Pheiffer. Carson's troops went to the west entrance of Canyon de Chelly, and Pheiffer's went to the east entrance. When they finally met in the canyon, they made the important discovery that the canyon actually had an additional branch. Their troops sang about their mission (Bailey 1988, 163):

"Come dress your ranks, my gallant souls,
a standing in a row,

Kit Carson is waiting to march
against the foe;
At night we march to Moqui,
o'er lofty hills of snow,
To meet and crush the savage foe,
bold Johnny Navajo,
Johnny Navajo! Johnny Navajo!"

The years 1863 and 1864 were devastating for the Diné. Because they were constantly on the move and unable to grow and store food, they began to capitulate by the hundreds at Fort Defiance and Fort Wingate. Although eventually several thousand Navajos took the Long Walk to Fort Sumner, many Navajos refused to do so and hid in the Grand Canyon, Navajo Mountain, and wherever else they could find refuge. (see Plate 11)

By the end of 1864 over eight thousand Navajos had surrendered and taken the Long Walk to Fort Sumner, a distance that ranged anywhere from 250 to 400 miles, depending on the point of origin. Because groups of Navajos surrendered at different times, many "long walks" actually occurred over the next few years as more and more Navajos gave up. (see Map 2)

By all accounts, the journey to Bosque Redondo was hard and humiliating for the Diné. Here is a description of one of them:

On March 4 more than two thousand Indians began their "Long Walk" from Canby to Fort Sumner, taking with them 473 horses and 3,000 sheep. Perhaps this group was lucky, for subsistence was dwindling at the posts in Navajoland; blankets were practically

Routes of the Long Walk, 1864–66

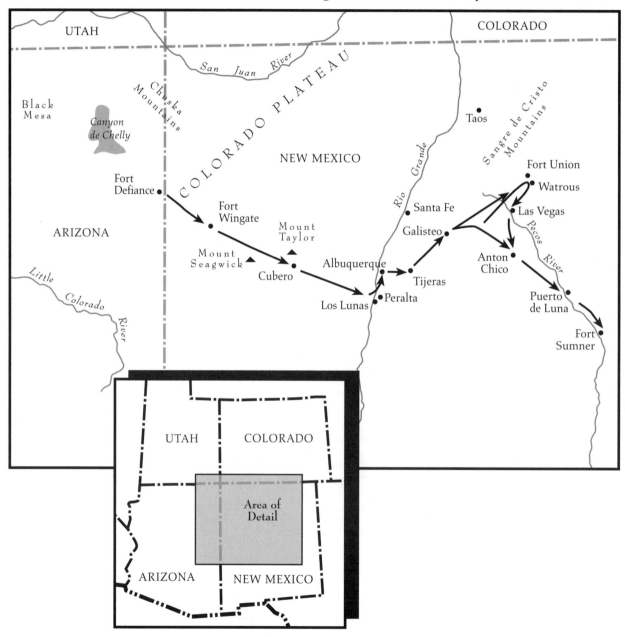

Map 2 Routes of the Long Walk, 1864–68, by Gary Tong.

non-existent and the results were inevitable. In little over a week's time 126 Navajos died of dysentery and exposure at Fort Canby. Flour had been furnished to those Indians leaving for Bosque Redondo without a word as how to prepare it for consumption. They ate it raw or mixed with water as a gruel. Unaccustomed to this type of fare, many doubled up with cramps of dysentery and crawled to the side of the road to perish. Those Navajos unable to resume their march were shot, perhaps mercifully, by their blue clad escorts. (Bailey 1988, 167–68)

Although many accounts have been given of the Long Walk, the most powerful stories are those retold by the Navajo elders who remember the hardship and humiliations of their incarceration. Curly Tso, a Navajo elder, recounts:

> On the journey to Hwééldi (Fort Sumner) the people had to walk. There were a few wagons to haul some personal belongings, but the trip was made on foot. People were shot down on the spot if they complained about being tired or sick, or if they stopped to help someone. If a woman became in labor with a baby, she was killed. There was absolutely no mercy. (Johnson 1973, 103–4)

Hundreds of other stories from the Navajo perspective document recollections just as powerful as this one.

Carleton promised the Diné that Fort Sumner would be a wonderful place to live, with plenty of food and materials for housing. This was not the case at all. As hard as the Navajos worked to irrigate and raise crops, they were unsuccessful. Insects destroyed their fields year after year. The water from the Pecos River caused dysentery. Wood was scarce, and as the years passed, the Navajo had to search farther and farther to find it. Many of the Navajo women were infected with diseases they caught from the soldiers at the fort. And to make matters worse, the Comanches became more and more brazen in their attacks on the fort and the Navajos. Starvation was rampant, so much so that desperate measures were taken to find food.

> The U.S. Army fed corn to its horses. Then, when the horses discharged undigested corn in their manure, the Diné would dig and poke in the manure to pick out the corn that had come back out. They could be seen poking around in every corral. They made the undigested corn into meal. Plenty of hot water was used with a very small amount of corn; and it was said that hot water was the strongest of all foods. The Diné spent four years at Fort Sumner living in a most miserable way. (Johnson 1973, 242)

The living conditions were equally abhorrent. Locke states:

> At Bosque Redondo each family unit

Figure 4
Counting Indians. Bosque Redondo Era, Fort Sumner, New Mexico, 1864–68. Courtesy of Museum of New Mexico, neg. no. NM 28534. Photographer unknown.

was given a plot of land to farm. Those that arrived too late to plant that spring helped others, usually clan relatives, dig irrigation ditches for fields of corn, melon squash and a large field of wheat that was being cultivated under the supervision of the soldiers. But there was never enough to eat and everyone was living in makeshift shelters, as materials were not available to construct hogans. Some families were living in holes they had dug in embankments, others had erected crooked poles and covered them with sheepskins. The families that had been rich back in Dinétah lived alongside those that had been poor, in the same sort of hovels, worked shoulder to shoulder with them scratching in the alkali-permeated soil and drank the bitter water from the Rio Pecos that made them ill. (Locke 1992, 364–65) (see Figures 4 and 5)

After a few years it became obvious that Carleton's experiment at Fort Sumner was an unqualified disaster. In September 1866 Carleton was relieved of his command. Even though the Bureau of Indian Affairs took control of Fort Sumner in January 1867, negotiations for the release of the Navajos did not begin until the spring of 1868. Colonel Samuel F. Tappan and General William Tecumseh Sherman worked with the Navajo headmen at Fort Sumner on a treaty. During these negotiations the Diné called upon the Holy People to assist them in their return to their homeland. According to Ruth Roessel, a Navajo elder:

Time and time again the Holy People came to the aid of the Navajos and are responsible for assisting them in returning home and being restored to their land. One reads the stories which relate to the coyote ceremony held at

Fort Sumner which, in the eyes of the tellers, was responsible for the change of heart in the Army that previously had refused to allow the Navajos to return home, but which, after the ceremony had been held, allowed the Diné to go back to their country. (Johnson 1973, xi)

It was during the meetings with Tappan

Figure 5
Navajo Woman and Baby. Bosque Redondo Era, Fort Sumner, New Mexico, 1864–68. Courtesy of Museum of New Mexico, neg. no. NM 3242. Photographer unknown.

and Sherman that the Navajo leader Barboncito said his famous words, "I hope to God you will not ask me to go anywhere except my own country. If we go back, we will follow whatever orders you give us. We do not want to go right or left, but straight back to our own land" (Sundberg 1995, 87). The Diné were blessed—on June 1, 1868, the Navajo and the United States of America signed a peace treaty. Although the Navajo received only one-fourth, or 3.5 million acres, of the original land they claimed, they were allowed to live among their four sacred mountains, a factor to which has been attributed their phenomenal growth. Before they started their journey home, a census and inventory was taken. There were 7,304 Navajos at Bosque Redondo when the treaty was signed. Two thousand of them had died of diseases such as smallpox, chicken pox, and pneumonia during their incarceration. In addition, nine hundred had escaped and several hundred were missing, which may be attributed to unreported deaths and slave kidnappings. Their livestock inventory tallied at 1,550 horses, 950 sheep, 1,025 goats, and 20 mules (Locke 1992, 383). (see Figure 6)

On June 18, 1868, the Diné started their return to their homeland. The procession was ten miles long and included soldiers from Fort Sumner, who protected them from attacks by other Native Americans as well as New Mexicans (Bailey 1988, 235).

On the return trip when the Diné saw Mount Taylor, their beloved sacred mountain to the south, they were overcome with emotion. Manuelito, a respected Navajo leader, exclaimed, "When we saw the top of the mountain from Albuquerque, we wondered if it was our mountain and we felt like talking to the ground, we loved it so" (Sundberg 1995, 78).

Once the Diné were back in their beloved country, they still had obstacles to overcome. The Navajo continued to be the target for livestock and slave raids. In addition, there was a food shortage. Many of the Diné lingered near the forts so that they could obtain food rations and be protected. The positive side of the situation was that the U.S. government made several significant promises to the Navajo in their treaty. The government promised to distribute livestock to the Navajo to replenish their supply of sheep and other animals and to provide education, one teacher per thirty Navajo children, for the Diné. Perhaps one of the most far-reaching side effects of the treaty was the fact that the Navajo were being treated as one people, one nation (Iverson 1990, 49).

Robert Roessel powerfully describes the resiliency of the Diné after their return from Fort Sumner: "Instead of being broken, crushed and bitter by this concentration camp experience the Navajos grew stronger and their roots went deeper. This increased strength of the Navajo in the face of such tribulation can be attributed mostly, perhaps entirely, to Navajo religion and to the faith and belief the Navajo people had in their Holy People. They never gave up" (R. A. Roessel 1980, 20).

Marilyn Help also has several stories about the Long Walk and her people's incarceration at Hwééldi, Fort Sumner.

One day someone mentioned Hwééldi, the Long Walk, to me and I did not know what they were talking about. So I asked my dad what it meant. He said,

Figure 6

Navajo, Barboncito, ca. 1868. Courtesy of National Anthropological Archives, Smithsonian Institution, neg. no. 55, 766.

"Hwééldi was when our people were driven together to make the Long Walk. Our people were starving and going through really hard times. It is kind of hard to talk about it because that was when bad things happened to our grandmothers and grandfathers. Things were so bad that our people had to take apart their deerskin moccasins and boil and eat them because they were so hungry. They also killed rats and cooked them for food because they were starving." Before the Long Walk our people had to hide in the mountains. It was one of the harshest things that could have happened. Our grandparents couldn't even build a fire because they feared that the soldiers might see the smoke. It is still hard for us to talk about that time because it is such a bad memory. We do not ever want to go through something like that again.

I have also heard the story about my grandfather, Hastiin Hataałí, a medicine man. When he was just a young boy, he got up early one morning and went over the side of a hill near his hogan. While he was there, he heard terrible noises from his home; the soldiers were killing his family. When he returned to his hogan, he discovered that his entire family had been murdered. After grabbing his rug blanket, he escaped to the Zuni people and herded sheep for them during the Long Walk years.

My grandmother went on the Long Walk to Hwééldi and survived her four years there. And my grandfather's sister told me that one of her aunts was captured as a slave, too (by the Mexicans). But she ran away and was on her way home when she was recaptured, this time by the soldiers, who made her go to Fort Sumner. I heard that when she was making her escape from the Mexicans, she sang songs in her traditional way and the owl helped her find her way back. There were also timber wolves and bears chasing them, and they had to sit in a tree for a long time until she could continue safely. Unfortunately, she was captured again and made the Long Walk.

I think the Diné performed ceremonies at Fort Sumner because we could have been forced to go to a reservation in Oklahoma; instead, we were allowed to come back here to our four sacred mountains. Sherman had a kind heart and let us come home.

Marilyn wrote a poem about the Long Walk and the Diné's captivity at Hwééldi.

It Is Said
Many years have passed since the tragic
moments of the "Long Walk."
"Grandmother,
I want to know about Hwééldi."
"It is said
Hwééldi is suffering and hardship.
Many soldiers gathered our people, who were
driven to the east like cattle and sheep,
Driven to a place unknown and unfamiliar.
"It is said

Many elderly, women,
and children died because of Hwééldi;
The elderly were left behind,
Pregnant women were taken behind rock
boulders and a short while later the sound of
a gunshot was heard.
"It is said
That starvation was so great, moccasins were
taken apart, boiled, and eaten.
Happiness did not happen, grandchild.

"It is said
When the Diné people were released,
it was a great day.
The Diné saw and recognized the peak
Mount Taylor and they wept;
I can hear the words of the ancient ones:
'Be strong.'
"It is said
Remember the Diné way."

-Marilyn Help

The Song Connection

*Although there is not universal agreement on the history and origin of "Shí Naashá,"
one widely accepted theory is that the song was created during the Long Walk period.
"Shí Naashá" beautifully expresses and affirms the Navajo belief in hózhǫ́ and their
joyous thanksgiving as they returned to their homeland between the four sacred
mountains.*

"Shí Naashá"
(I Am Going)

Background Information

According to what I know, they say that this song was made to remember the Long Walk. The words in the song mean that you have a feeling for yourself that you are going to survive, that you are special, and that you are going to live a long life. You are thinking about yourself and your self-respect. That is what this song is about. I learned this song from my dad. He used to sing it to us. There are other words to the song that talk about a long life and the rainbow path road that I walk. I added motions to the song because it was the only way I could get my children at school motivated to learn it. They really enjoy doing things with their hands and their feet and dancing.

This song is probably a Circle Dance. Even though I have never seen the Circle Dance done with "Shí Naashá," it can probably be done with it. I met a man who revised the song and added new lyrics to it. He said that he is glad that the song was being used to educate children. He said that he added new lyrics to the song because of how our people suffered for so long in Hwééldi [Fort Sumner]. One time they were doing a movie and wanted him to do a dedication in Window Rock and he said that is when he added more lyrics to the song. His first name is Arthur Yazzie, and in our traditional way he would be my "son." [Marilyn is referring to the clan system used by the Diné.] He is very old and lives in Mexican Springs, just northwest of where I live.

In the notes that accompany the Folkways recording *Music of the Sioux and the Navajo*, musicologist Willard Rhodes cites the genesis of the song: "This song was sung by the women to sustain the morale and hope of the men during the confinement of the Navajo at Fort Sumner following their capitulation to Kit Carson in 1864" (Rhodes 1953, 5). Kay Bennett, Navajo singer and author, agrees that this song first appeared among the Diné during the Fort Sumner period. She suggests, however, that it was written when her people were released from their captivity. On her record notes for one of her recordings, *Kaibah*, she states, "It is believed that this was one of the songs the Navajo people sang after being released from the concentration camp in 1868." Her version of the words to "Shí Naashá" has several verses, including

> I am walking about in beauty.
> I walk with corn pollen.
> I walk beneath the rainbow.

Whether or not the song is over a hundred years old and originated during the Long Walk, there is a consensus that "Shí Naashá" is a beautiful Navajo secular song. Ruth Roessel, Navajo singer, author, and educator, says that "Shí Naashá" is a good song to teach because it is a special song that can "easily be picked up." Marilyn Help agrees with this conclusion. She said that it is an authentic Navajo song because so many of the Diné sing it and know it. It is perfect for non-Navajos to learn since it has so many lovely words in it and projects a feeling of beauty. She sings "Shí Naashá" frequently when she performs in schools, thereby fulfilling her objective of using traditional music of the Diné to enhance her students' self-esteem, to keep the Navajo culture alive, and to acknowledge and celebrate Navajo traditions. Leroy Morgan, a Navajo educator, laughingly describes this song as the one that all of the beauty pageant contestants sing. Although these Navajo educators have not seen "Shí Naashá" performed at an Enemy-way ceremony, they agree that it could be danced and sung as part of the Squaw Dance.

Information about the music

After an eight-beat introduction on the drum, Marilyn sings the vocables, "hee yee' yąą ą," on the tonic note, or home tone. With the exception of one passing note, the melody outlines the tonic triad throughout the song. The middle section of the song illustrates a descending melodic line that starts high and then gradually drops to the tonic. There is a strong feeling of the beat subdivided into threes. This type of rhythmic movement is often found in songs that are used for Circle

Dances (McAllester 1992, 37). The Diné perform Circle Dances at the Enemyway ceremony. Like the Two-step and Skip, they are part of the Squaw Dance repertoire. "Shí Naashá" fits the criteria for a Circle Dance performance (McAllester and Mitchell 1983, 609). As with other Navajo songs, the meter changes to accommodate the text.

Experiencing the music

An effective way to learn the song "Shí Naashá" is to identify and practice singing the vocables at the introduction (*"hee yee' yąą' ą'"*), interlude (*"hee ya hee nee ya'"*), and ending (*"hee ya hee nee ya'"*). Once these parts are mastered, try to sing the first two phrases that are repeated, *"ahala ahalágó naashá gh̨a, ahala ahalágó naashá gh̨a."* Finally, practice the middle section.

A Circle Dance may be performed with "Shí Naashá." The underlying feeling of the music is a subdivision of the beat into threes. Therefore the basic dance step is a long (beats 1 and 2)/short (beat 3) movement. Dancers join hands in a circle formation and move clockwise to the beat. The left foot moves on the long part of the beat and the right foot follows on the short part. In addition, the dancers subtly move their hands inward and outward as they perform. They also join in and sing with the music. The drummer stands outside the circle and accompanies the song with a steady beat.

The Diné sing "Shí Naashá" throughout the year as a social song. If it is sung and danced as part of the Squaw Dance repertoire, however, the Enemyway time strictures need to be honored.

Interlinear Translation

Ahala	(freedom, in the way of the freedom)
gó	(in the way of)
naa	(around)
shá	(I go)
ghạ	(really)
Shí	(I)
naa	(around)
shá	(I go)
ghạ	(really)
lago	(in the way of)
hózhǫ́ǫ́	(beauty)
lá	(really)
ládéé	(right in front)

Translation

Ahala ahalágó naashá ghạ.	I am going in freedom.
Shí naashá ghạ, shí naashá ghạ,	I am going in beauty all around me.
shí naashá lago hózhǫ́ǫ́ lá.	
Shí naashá ghạ, shí naashá ghạ,	I am going, I am going, in beauty;
shí naashá, ládéé hózhǫ́ǫ́ lá.	it is around me.

Note: Marilyn has created motions to the song "Shí Naashá" (see Appendix B.)

Shí Naashá
(I Am Going)

drum

Hee yee' yaa' a'

A-ha-la, a-ha-lá-gó naa-shá gha, a-ha-la, a-ha-lá-gó naa-shá gha,

Shí naa-shá gha, shí naa-shá gha, shí naa-shá la-go hó-zhǫǫ lá,
(2x) lá-deé

hee ya hee nee ya', A-ha-la, a-ha-lá-gó naa-shá gha,

a-ha-la, a-ha-lá-gó naa-shá gha, Shí naa-shá gha, shí naa-shá gha,

shí naa-shá la-go hó-zhǫǫ lá, hee ya hee nee ya'.

Chapter 6

THE MEANING OF CORN

The Song . . .

"Náá' diishoh"
(Brush Off the Corn)

Close inspection of a traditional Navajo wedding basket often reveals remnants of cornmeal or corn pollen, a sacred food of the Diné. The use of corn, in many of its forms, appears frequently in Navajo ceremonies and has a long history among the Navajo. As with many other aspects of Navajo culture, the Holy People explain its significance in the creation story. During the First World, or Black World, two clouds, the Black Cloud and the White Cloud, merged in the east. A vague, misty image of First Man was created from them, as well as a perfectly formed ear of white corn. In the West the Yellow Cloud and the Blue Cloud joined to create First Woman, who also appeared as an indefinite form, a "Misty Being." She held a perfectly shaped ear of yellow corn (O'Bryan 1956, 1–2).

Another reference to corn in the evolution tale is an event that occurred in the Fourth World. Locke cites that when the inhabitants of the Fourth World were traveling to the Fifth World, the Kisani (Pueblo) remembered to bring an ear of corn with them. Because both the Kisani and Navajo wanted the corn, they split it into halves: the Kisani got the "butt," or good part, and the Navajo got the tip, only to have Coyote run away with it. This story explains why the Pueblo people have always had more successful and plentiful corn harvests than the Diné (Locke 1992, 76).

The function of corn in traditional Navajo life is both practical and spiritual. It serves the utilitarian purpose of providing the Diné with food and nutrition for themselves and their livestock. Corn also has ritualistic import: it connects the Diné with the Holy People through its use in prayers and ceremonies. Kluckhohn and Leighton observe this bond: "The use of pollen of corn and other plants is very important in maintaining the proper relationship to the Holy People. In old-fashioned households the day still begins with the sprinkling of pollen from one of the little bags and a murmured prayer. After the evening meal the members of the family rub their limbs and say, 'May I be lively, May I be healthy.' More pollen may be offered and a Blessing Way song sung" (Kluckhohn and Leighton 1974, 203).

Marilyn Help refers to this idea in her explanation of the relevance of corn to the Diné:

Corn is really important because it is used in our ceremonies all of the time, as well as for our food. The reason why it is so special is because the Holy People were the ones who presented the corn to us so that we could use it in many ways. When you say your prayers, there is a certain part where you say "Naadą́ą́' Ałgai Ashkii [White Corn Boy], Naadą́ą́' Ałtsoi At'ééd [Yellow Corn Girl]." There is male, white corn and female, yellow corn. In the morning when you pray, you sprinkle the white corn pollen

to the east and the yellow corn pollen to the west. In our traditional Navajo way, the corn sides are always straight across from each other, male and female. We believe that everything in our lives and surroundings is either male or female, facing each other. For example, even in electricity there is a male or female component.

There is only one type of corn pollen that comes off the corn. At the very tip of the stalk there are tassels at the end. When our corn is ripe with corn pollen, we shake it early in the morning to gather the pollen in a big pan. The corn pollen is always yellow. Whether or not there is color in the corn, the pollen is yellow. When you pray with corn pollen, you dip your finger into the corn pollen bag and then put your finger with the corn pollen on the tip of your tongue and then the top of your head. Then you spread it toward the earth and say a prayer. That is how we always do it. We always put it on our tongue and then on the top of our head. That is exactly how we were taught.

The Holy People always want us to use corn pollen in this way because we are respecting our surroundings, our Mother Earth. We are thankful to Mother Earth, and she appreciates it when we say our prayers with corn pollen like that. Corn pollen may be used anytime during the day and for ceremonies. You can also use white cornmeal to the east in the morning when you say your prayers and yellow

Figure 7
A newly planted cornfield, sheep, and scarecrow at Marilyn Help's home in Tolakai, New Mexico.

cornmeal to the west when the sun is going down. I collect corn pollen all of the time and put it in my corn pollen bag.

When there is a Hózhǫ́ǫ́jí, I take it to be blessed by the medicine man because then it will have power and energy.

Although many of the prescribed traditional methods for planting corn are no longer practiced, it is not unusual for Navajos who follow the Diné way to say prayers for its plentiful harvest. For example, Marilyn Help and her family grow their own corn on a small patch of land near their home. When she plants her corn, she says prayers and throws corn pollen into the field, thereby encouraging it to grow in a healthy way so that it may produce other good things. (see Figure 7)

Another practice that is less frequently performed is the ritual of feeding a newborn infant corn pollen (Kluckhohn and Leighton 1974, 207). Although Marilyn acknowledges that this act may still be practiced, she believes it is more common for mothers to have a Blessingway performed before their children are born. Because the mother eats corn pollen during this ceremony, the baby in her womb will have eaten it, too, through its nourishment from the mother's body.

Marilyn notes an additional use of corn in her culture: the Diné perform a Blessingway for sheep. As part of this ritual, they feed a selected sheep corn pollen before they butcher one of its kind. They believe that this act will increase their livestock in a healthy and harmonious manner. Then they take a piece of wool from the sheep they will slaughter and throw it into the sheep corral so that it knows that its life will end in order to supply the needs of the family.

Corn is also a significant part of Kinaaldá,

the traditional Navajo puberty ceremony designed for adolescent girls when they have their first menstruation. Marilyn did not have her Kinaaldá performed because her family procrastinated in making the arrangements for it. She still regrets this decision and realizes the importance of tying a girl's hair with deerskin right away, which initiates the start of the ceremony. According to Monty Roessel, it was not unusual for women who went through adolescence in the 1950s and 1960s to miss their Kinaaldás. He explains:

> In the 1950s and 1960s, the Kinaaldá ceremony almost died. It was a time when most Navajo children were taken away from their families by the United States government and sent to boarding schools. At these schools, Navajos were punished for speaking their own language. The only time they were allowed to come home was for the summer. The children did not spend much time with the elders who knew the Kinaaldá and other ceremonies. As a result, the ceremonies were performed less and less often. Young girls were growing up without having the Kinaaldá. Some families forgot how to perform it. (M. Roessel 1993, 28)

Marilyn's daughters, Shannon and Joni, have had their Kinaaldás. They both said that during the morning on the last day of the ceremony they could feel changes within them, as if they were turning into women with new sources of energy.

As with most of the traditional Navajo ceremonies, the history of the Kinaaldá is traced to the creation story. Changing Woman, or White Shell Woman, had the very first Kinaaldá, a special ceremony that honors women, the child bearers who replenish the human race. Although the ceremony has many fascinating components, one of the most intriguing has to do with corn. On the next-to-last day of the two- to four-day ceremony, the young woman grinds corn for a corn cake and then blesses and shares it with all participants who attend her ceremony. Although the traditional way was to have the girl grind the corn by hand, using her grinding stone, it is not uncommon to use ready-made cornmeal today. The girl must bless the cornmeal, too. She has to work hard to stir and combine all of the ingredients for the corn cake. Before the cake is baked, it is surrounded by corn husks that the girl has sewn together by hand. She takes corn pollen from a traditional Navajo wedding basket and sprinkles it in a prescribed manner over the cake. After baking all night in a specially prepared outdoor underground oven, the cake is ready to eat. Early the next morning she serves each guest and refrains from eating a piece herself because of her sensitive physical state.

Since the use of corn intertwines so many aspects of Navajo culture, it is no wonder that the corn harvest is an important event for Marilyn and her family. At times their corn is so plentiful, it seems that there might even be too much. Nevertheless, none of it can be wasted. Part of the corn is thrown into a pit, steamed, and dried. The rest of it is cleaned and put into barrels for storage. Corn is always in demand and must be saved because young Navajo girls are always coming of age for their Kinaaldá. Marilyn also saves their corn husks to wrap their tobacco for mountain smokes. She continually gathers corn pollen, preferably in the early morning, when the wind is not blowing and it is serene and quiet.

The Diné use corn in a multitude of ways to commune with and honor the Holy People—it is an integral part of the Navajo world. The expression, "the corn pollen rule" beautifully symbolizes the traditional culture of the Diné in its reminder to the People to live the Navajo way.

The Song Connection

The Diné sing special corn-grinding songs to make the laborious task of grinding corn less tedious. When Marilyn grinds corn, she uses the mano, tsé deeshch'įní, and metate, tsé deeshjee', that have belonged to her family for several generations.

"Náá' diishoh"
(Brush Off the Corn)

Background Information

My dad is the one who taught me this song. In fact, he taught me almost all of the songs that I know. This one is kind of like a "song act" that you can do. It is sung when we show a typical Navajo scene for our programs. You bring out all of your corn-grinding stones, sheep hide, and goat hide for the program. People tie their hair back in a Navajo knot, and you have an aunt or somebody holding a baby and rocking the baby back and forth when people are singing. It is a social song where everybody can get involved. It is a traditional song for corn grinding and is sung to make the baby stop crying.

You make a corn-grinding sound with the corn-grinding stones when you sing. And there is a certain place where you stop and brush off the corn; you sweep it off. First you put the corn on top of the grindstone and then you kind of just go up and down like this to crush it. Then you start going back and forth, back and forth. It has to be an even motion. And sometimes if you are used to it, you can go up again and then go back down like this and then back and forth, back and forth. There are two stones, basically. I have the stones at my house. My grandma on my father's side gave me her corn-grinding stone, and I still have it from a long time ago. She was my nálí. Her name was Asdzą́ą́ Hashk'aan, Yucca Fruit Strung in a Line

Clan. That is what she was called. That was her name. (see Plate 12)

Corn-grinding songs are easily identified by the Diné because of characteristic rhythmic patterns. When the singer starts the song with a variant of the rhythmic formula (see Figure 8), the experienced listener knows that a corn-grinding song is about to be sung (McAllester and Mitchell 1983, 617; Johnson 1964, 105; Rhodes 1987, 12). Although these songs were originally sung to accompany and make easier the laborious task of grinding corn, they are also performed as social songs. According to Johnson's Navajo informants, corn and wheat grinding was a cooperative effort by many women in the "old days." She states, "Those doing the grinding, always women, would form a line facing East with their grindstones in front of them resting on a goat or sheep skin. The woman at the north end would begin and the results of her grinding would be passed in a basket to the woman on her right. As the corn traveled down the line, it would be progressively finer" (Johnson 1964, 102). Rhodes observes that both Navajo men and women sing corn-grinding songs and perform the task of grinding corn (Rhodes 1987, 12). He also notes that as with many components of traditional Navajo culture, the Diné acknowledge the Holy People: "Before beginning the grinding of the corn, white cornmeal was offered to the gods and was ceremonially thrown or sprinkled on the heads, front, back, sides, and top of the singers and grinders" (Rhodes 1987, 12).

Johnson observes that ground meal was also used in a more frivolous way: "It was customary after each song for the women and men to 'exchange compliments' by sprinkling each other with a bit of ground corn. Either side could initiate the action which caused considerable hilarity" (Johnson 1964, 102). The lyrics of the songs were often cause for levity, too (Johnson 1964, 102, and Rhodes 1987, 12).

Information about the music

In her 1964 study of Navajo corn-grinding songs, Johnson cites several musical characteristics that make this genre of songs identifiable. These include (1) a melodic range of an octave or more that may start low and then rise with a gradual descent to the tonic; (2) an emphasis on the tonic, third, fourth, and fifth scale degrees; (3) multiple meters (duple and triple); (4) from four to six different melodic phrases; and (5) an identifiable "metrical-musical form," as noted above (Johnson 1964, 104). The corn-grinding song sung by Marilyn, "Náá' diishoh," fits many of the musical characteristics outlined by Johnson. "Náá' diishoh" begins with the rhythmic pattern described by Johnson (1964), McAllester

Figure 8
Characteristic rhythmic formula for Navajo corn-grinding songs.

and Mitchell (1983), and Rhodes (1987). The melody starts on the tonic and then leaps an octave higher, gradually working its way down to the tonic once again. Additional musical characteristics that support Johnson's analysis are: the main melodic notes are the tonic, third, fourth, and fifth; there are frequent metrical shifts; and the melody has at least six different musical phrases in addition to two distinctive vocable patterns.

Experiencing the music

The words show a secondary function of the grinding song: to keep a baby entertained and happy. Marilyn sings, "Baby is crying. Hurry and grind. Why are you fussy while grinding the corn?" Johnson observes that the reference to a baby in grinding songs is common. She states:

Babies are as important in these songs as the actual grinding. It is easy to imagine them in their cradle boards watching the teasing and general hilarity, and adding their crying to the urging of the singers that the women hurry and finish. (Johnson 1964, 107)

Johnson also makes a connection between fertility and grinding corn. Kinaaldá, the traditional Navajo rite of passage from girlhood to womanhood, uses corn grinding as an integral part of the ritual (ibid., 208).

Marilyn sings this song as she grinds corn with her mano, *tsé deeshch'įní*, on the metate, *tsé deeshjee'*. The recurring beat of this song and hypnotic vocables compel the listener to imitate the corn-grinding movements. These motions are described in Appendix C.

Interlinear Translation

Náá'	(again)
diishoh	(brush it)
Awéé'	(baby)
yichaoo	(crying)
Tsxįįłgo	(in a hurry)
ník'áó	(grind)
Háásh	(how)
díiłíílgo	(while making)
saał	(angry words)
ník'áó	(grind)

Translation

Náá'diishoh.	Brush off the corn.
Awéé' yichaoo.	Baby is crying.
Tsxįįłgo ník'áó.	Hurry and grind.
Háásh díiłíílgo saał ník'áó?	Why are you fussy while grinding the corn?

Náá' diishoh
(Brush Off the Corn)

drum

Ee ya- he- ya, ee ya-he-ya, Ha- loo shee yee wee-se-loo, ha-loo

shee yee wee-se-loo we-se-loo, ha-loo shee yee wee-se-laa,
2x (loo)
Fine

'oo wee 'oo wo 'ee yee náá' dii-shoh, e-ya-he-ya-he aa' a' a-we a-we.

A-wéé' yi-chao - o, a-wéé' yi-chao - o, a-wéé' yi-chao - o,

Yoo' oo náá' dii-shoh, yoo' oo náá' dii-shoh, Tsxįį́ł-go nik'-ao wee yaa he',

e-ya-he-ya-he aa' a' a-we a-we, Háásh dii-łíił-go saał nik'- ao wee yaa he',

e-ya-he-ya-he aa' a' a-we a-we, Yoo' oo náá' dii-shoh, yoo' oo náá' dii-shoh,

D.S. al Fine

yoo' oo, Tsxįį́ł-go nik'-ao wee yaa he, e-ya-he-ya-he aa' a' a-we a-we.

Chapter 7

MUSIC OF THE DINÉ

The Song . . .

"Aniid Nannáádą́ą́ga'"
(When You Were Young)

A listener unfamiliar with Navajo music might conjure up a Hollywood stereotype image of Native Americans dancing around a fire in colorful regalia to the beat (*one*, two, three, four; *one*, two, three, four) of a drum. The power of the media is very persuasive and pervasive. But although music is an integral part of Navajo ceremonies, it is unique in its variety and complexity, contradicting the Hollywood myth of a "universal" American Indian sound. Navajo music includes traditional ceremonial and social songs of the past as well as contemporary music. Whether old or new, sacred or social, many Navajos believe that all of their music is ultimately a gift from the Holy People and treat it with respect.

Ceremonial and social songs constitute the traditional Navajo music repertoire. Because of the healing power associated with ceremonial songs and chants, the Diné rarely perform them out of context. If they are sung inappropriately, the Holy People may cause harm to befall the singer. There are also strictures on the performance time for certain ceremonies. For example, as stated in chapter 1, traditional Navajos only sing and dance the social music from the Enemyway, a ceremony that purifies and protects the patient, between the first thunder of spring and the first frost of winter. Medicine persons conduct the Nightway exclusively in the wintertime. More detailed information on ceremonial songs, chants, and instruments is provided in chapter 4, on hózhǫ́ and rituals.

Any time of the year, the Diné sing social songs that do not have a ritual connection. These may include but are not limited to songs about occupations or tasks, such as corn-grinding songs, humorous songs, and songs about animals. There are also powerful social songs, games, and stories that demand special use. For example, the Diné honor the Holy People by singing moccasin game songs, playing string games, and telling Coyote tales only in the wintertime. Although these time strictures are an old tradition, they are still upheld by many Navajos today.

In addition to traditional Navajo music, the reverberations of contemporary American music culture abound on the reservation. It is not unusual to attend a Navajo Song and Dance Contest and simultaneously hear a pop rock performance by young Navajos in one area, in stark contrast to the music of a traditional Skip Dance in another. The Diné listen to all kinds of music: country-western, rock, pop, jazz, and classical. One can purchase recordings of Navajo gospel singers, rock performers, and country-western artists in addition to traditional social song tape cassettes and compact discs. Far from stereotypical, Navajo music is a constantly changing genre that includes both traditional and contemporary styles. But since the focus of this book is on conventional aspects of Navajo culture, only traditional ceremonial and social song char-

acteristics are examined in this chapter, starting with a look at the word *music*.

Although *music* does not appear in every English-Navajo dictionary, it has a Navajo name: *hataał* (singing). In fact, there are Navajo words for many musical terms, such as song, *sin;* drum, *ásaa'* (pot) *yilghaałi* (hitting); tuba, *dilni* (sound) *heeneezgo* (in an elongated sound); ukulele, *agaanstsiin* (forearm) *yilązhi* (pluck) *yázhi* (small); and synthesizer, *Dilni* (sounds) *Bee* (with) *Naagizi* (turning), to mention a few (Parnwell 1989, 98–99). Ceremonial and social songs also have specific Navajo terms. According to McAllester and Mitchell, *hatáál sin* refers to ceremonial songs. *Diné biyiin,* a category that technically may include any song, is the most commonly used term to describe social songs (McAllester and Mitchell 1983, 605).

McAllester and Mitchell outline the musical characteristics of traditional Navajo music in the *Handbook of North American Indians:*

1. Voice: robust and nasal with subtle ornamental grace-notes and quavers. Range is medium for women: men often sing in the same range, which gives a high tenor or a piercing falsetto effect.
2. Melody: after an introductory formula on the tonic, or base note, the melody leaps up a fifth, octave or higher, then sweeps downward, often reaching the tonic again at the end of every phrase.
3. Formulas: There is an introductory formula that is often specific to a particular song style. It may be repeated as a

cadence at the ends of many phrases and it usually concludes the song. The effect is to give song styles an unusual consistency and clear-cut identity.

4. Scale: tone systems are heavily weighted and often limited to the tonic, the third, and the fifth (and the tonic again an octave higher). This emphasis on the triad is also a feature of Apache music and seems to occur in Northern Athapaskan music as well. It is not frequent in other American Indian music.

5. Note Values: prevailingly limited to two, the eighth and the quarter note, throughout Navajo traditional music.

6. Meter: usually duple with interest added by means of an occasional extra beat. A few styles use a triple meter.

7. Text: usually brief meaningful texts surrounded by vocables. . . . Older texts may be composed entirely of vocables. Ceremonial chants differ strongly from this in that they contain many lines of narrative poetry (McAllester and Mitchell 1983, 606).

With a few exceptions, the twelve songs in this book adhere to these musical characteristics. One exception is vocal timbre, or tone color. Although a listener may hear a nasalized singing style on recordings and in live performances of traditional Navajo singers, many Navajos sing with a more contemporary vocal sound. For example, Marilyn Help has a free and open-throated singing voice, with only an occasional tightness in her throat on selected notes. Vocal timbres in Navajo songs depend on the singer and the type of song being sung. The songs in this book do have the following musical characteristics described by McAllester and Mitchell. With one or two exceptions, the melodies of each tune start low, followed by an upward melodic movement that gradually goes down again. They also have vocables (words that are integral to the song but have no exact translations, like *la*) in distinctive patterns at the beginning and ending of each song and sometimes in the interludes. Several songs consist entirely of vocables. The scale patterns frequently outline a triad and emphasize the tonic, or home tone. In addition, the note values are predominately quarter and two-eighths. The meter in these twelve songs changes frequently, however, because of the text. If an extra word or two of text is added, the meter changes to accommodate it.

Another musical characteristic of these songs is the use of instruments, for example, rattles, the basket drum, and the bull-roarer at ceremonies (see chapter 4). Singers play a water drum to accompany the Enemyway social songs and dances. Navajos also use other types of drums for song accompaniment. Marilyn accompanies eleven songs included in this book with a drum that her brother gave her. It is a two-headed drum with a wooden resonating chamber shaped like a barrel. Deer hide is used for the drumhead, mallet, and string that connects the two drumheads together. Each song resonates with the sound of the steady, recurring drumbeat, connecting Marlyn Help with her traditional past. (see Figure 9)

Marilyn Help has sung the songs of her people since she was a small child. She describes her musical experiences.

My dad is the one who has taught me my songs. I have also picked up some songs here and there. But the main ones, like the ceremonial songs, I learned from my dad. I've learned some of the social songs from him, and others I've learned on my own.

Figure 9
The two-headed drum that is heard on the recording.

I can remember one time when my dad taught us a song. It was at night and we were in the hogan, during the wintertime. It was kind of cute because he started singing a Yeibichai song (from the Nightway ceremony) and he said, "Follow me, follow me, now everybody get behind me." We were all dancing and going after him. I remember that we were just little, but we all really got involved. He was singing, and my mom was laughing and laughing, she thought it was so funny. That was one cute thing I remember about singing a song with my family.

Music is integral to the Navajo world. I think that most parents want their children to learn traditional Navajo music. I teach it at the school where I work, and so far, the majority of parents are really impressed and pleased with what we're doing, especially trying to promote the Navajo language.

There are Navajo songs that everyone sings, children and adults. I think that most of them are pretty good for kids, except for ceremonial songs that are sacred, like songs about White Shell Woman and Monster Slayer. But there are certain songs from the Holy People that we sing in the wintertime when we tell the winter tales. Then we may sing songs about the animals and animal people and how they used to sing in the wintertime. Like when they did the shoe game for the children; those are the songs that you sing for them, and they really like that. They sit there and listen and listen and listen, even though some of them understand only English and very few understand Navajo. I have to keep going back and forth, back and forth with English and Navajo just to clarify things. My students will sit there and listen so attentively, you could hear a pin drop in the room when I was talking. Our children are really hungry for this kind of teaching; they want to know who they are. They want to know their traditional ways. It's amazing. My students give me goose bumps when they are like that because they are really learning the Diné way.

Sometimes a song comes to me in my dream on its own. I have to remember it, so I subconsciously keep telling myself, "You have to remember this tune, you have to remember this song." I think the Holy People have a lot to do with it. They have given me the gift of singing, and I am glad to receive it. I want to sing for people, and when I do, I want to be good, but I also want to be humble. So I try to keep myself at a level where I have humility. Because of that, the Holy People have given me this gift. I am glad I sing for people. That is how I feel about it.

My good-luck songs are the ceremonial songs that my dad taught me, especially the ones about Whispering God. They call them Haashch'e'ewąąn. These are good-luck songs because they are sung in a real sacred way. That is the path I want to walk, hózhǫ́ǫ́jí. Those are the songs that I want to sing.

Whether traditional or contemporary, Navajo music offers a wide palette of sound for the listener. Music connects the Diné with the Holy People through the ceremonial songs and chants that have been performed for centuries.

The authors of this book request that the songs and dances presented in these chapters be performed with respect and in accordance with the time strictures mandated by the Holy People.

The Song Connection

Although any of the twelve songs in this book contribute to an understanding of Navajo music, "Anįįd Nannááda̜a̜ga'," When You Were Young, illustrates the intriguing phenomenon of receiving a song in a dream. Marilyn believes that this song is a gift to her from the Holy People. She joyously shares it with others. In addition, Marilyn says that this song sends a message about how to behave properly: Don't be conceited, and live with humility.

"Anįįd Nannááda̜a̜ga'"
(When You Were Young)

Background Information

This is a song that came to me in a dream. I had a dream about it, and I remember that I was telling myself in my dream that I had to remember the tune. And so when I woke up, I made sure that I sang the tune and that it was the right one. It still was the right one, and so that is why I remembered it. I kept singing it over and over that whole day until I really learned it well. And now it is on this tape. This is a new song. I think that the Holy People gave me this song as a gift when I was asleep, dreaming. When you dream like this, it really means something because a lot of times things that will happen in the future will be told to you in your dream. All of a sudden I was just dreaming about this song, and when I woke up, I wanted to just sing it, repeat it over and over so that I could remember it. And so that is what I did.

You can do a dance with this song. My children know it, too. My students do not know this song yet, but they do know how to perform the Two-step and the Skip.

This song can be taught to children because it has a moral teaching. The man in the song was conceited right from the beginning. And now, all of a sudden, old age has humbled him. We tease about the relationships between men and women, the "opposition" all of the time. I think that for me, personally, it keeps people in line because that way you don't begin to look down on people. And at the same time it is just like our Coyote stories that we have in our *Hajíínéí*, the beginning. The coyote is always there so that he can remind people of the trickster part of us human beings. We have to know when to limit ourselves to certain types of behavior, like stealing and other, different things that we are not supposed to do. That is what it brings out, not to laugh about the old people, not to laugh about people that are handicapped. There are moral teachings for us.

I could sing this song at a Song and Dance Contest, but I have not done it yet. It could also be sung at the Enemyway. I am happy to share this song with others. It is there for people to sing.

"When You Were Young" reflects the humor and teasing spirit that the Diné capture in many of their numerous Squaw Dance songs. Although Marilyn did not have a specific man in mind when she created this song, she enjoys the truth and moral tale expressed in the lyrics.

This is the only Skip Dance song in the book. As mentioned, the Skip and Two-step are two of the social dances the Diné perform at the Enemyway ceremony. The public is invited to participate in them as well. Although it may be challenging to the novice listener to aurally recognize the difference between the Two-step and the Skip, with repeated hearings it becomes easier. When in doubt, look at the other dancers and follow their lead. In general, the Two-step has a slower and more stately beat. The Skip has a faster tempo, which allows the dancers to use a heel-toe, toe-heel, or high "skip" movement.

Information about the music

The vocable pattern *hee yee yee yee yąą' ą'* occurs repeatedly in Marilyn's song "When You Were Young." It acts as a cadence, or closure, to almost every phrase in the melody. But several other vocable patterns are also integral to the song. The frequently used opening vocables *hee yee' yąą' ą'* start the song and introduce the music. In addition, a set of vocables surrounds the translatable words of the text, *"We yaa naa naa ei yoo'oo, we yaa naa naa ei yoo we'oo o-wee a, hee yee yee yee yąą' ą'."* The ending formula, *"hee yee yee yee ya we ya,"* is typical and recognizable to the Diné dancer. It signals to the dancers that the piece is about to end.

The majority of notes in the melody are the tonic, second, and third. In fact, the interplay between them provides the basis for the tune as they move in steps and skips within the range of a major third. The melody occasionally jumps to the fifth and sixth notes of the scale but soon descends to the tonic.

Although the beat of the song stays steady, the listener can distinguish changing meters, and the fast tempo of this song provides a compelling feeling of forward motion. The majority of note values are quarter and eighth notes. A syncopated pattern of eighth, quarter, eighth gives life to the piece.

Experiencing the music

This song provides an excellent illustration of the traditional Navajo Skip Dance. Females choose male partners, join hands with them as couples, and move clockwise around the circle. The Skip Dance has a variety of steps. Dancers may move to the beat using a heel-toe, toe-heel, or exaggerated skip motion. The Diné perform the heel-toe movement by placing their heel on the floor, toes pointing upward, on the first drumbeat. On the second drumbeat, the dancer slides the toe downward, back into place on the floor.

The second option, toe-heel, starts with the toe touching the floor, heel raised, on the first drumbeat. On the second drumbeat, the toe slides backward and the heel touches the floor. Dancers also perform the Skip Dance with an exaggerated alternate lifting of their knees, then a quick downward motion of the foot to the floor.

All of these dance steps are part of the traditional Navajo Skip Dance. The choice of dance step depends on each set of partners. Performers often follow the lead dancers and perform the step they model. But each set of partners ultimately decides what to do—all of the dancers don't have to move to the same step at the same time.

The terms designated for the dance steps—Two-step, and Skip Dance—depend on the locale of the performers. But the tempo of the music is the ultimate factor and criterion in the decision of which dance step to perform.

Interlinear Translation

Aniįd	(young)
nannáádą́ą́	(you walking around)
ga'	(in the past)
doo	(not)
shi	(me)
nóoł'įį́	(you looked at it)
Áłt'ą́ą́	(now)
ga'	(really)
są́	(old)
béé	(with)
níyáago	(when I arrived)
gá	(really)
T'óó	(just)
ga'	(really)
shích'į́į́	(toward me)
náá	(again)
náádlóóh'ó	(you smile)
łeh	(usually)

Translation

Aniid nannáádą́ą́ga', doo shinóoł'íí.

When you were young,
you never looked at me.

Áłt'ą́ą́ga' są béé níyáago gá-á,
T'óógá' shích'įį́ náánáádlóóh'ó (łeh).

Now when you become old,
You will be smiling at me (usually).

Aniįd Nannáádą́ągá'
(When You Were Young)

drum

Hee yee' yąą' ą', We yaa naa naa ei yoo' oo,

we yaa naa naa ei yoo we' oo o - wee a, hee yee yee yee yąą' ą',

We yaa naa naa ei yoo' oo, we yaa naa naa ei yoo we' oo o - wee a,

hee yee yee yee yąą' ą', we yaa naa naa ei yoo we' oo o - wee a,

hee yee yee yee yąą' ą', We yaa naa naa ei yoo' oo,

we yaa naa naa ei yoo we' oo o - wee a, hee yee yee yee yąą' ą', A-

nįįd nan - náá - dą́ą - ga' doo shi-noo1' - į́ - į́ ei yee yee

ei ya hee yoo' oo o - wee ya, hee yee yee yee yąą' ą', Áłt'-

Chapter 8

NAVAJO CLANS

The Song . . .

"Yo'oo' Eidoo-o' Hee Yee"
(A Dance Song)

Although *Navajo* and *Diné* are the two names most frequently used to describe the People, the next layer of their identity is the traditional clan system. Traditional Navajos introduce themselves by saying their name and then their clan relationship of their mother's side, "born of," followed by their clan relationship of their father's side, "born for." This immediately creates a point of reference for other Navajos; is this person my relative by clan or not? Even when two or more Navajos meet off the Navajo Nation, they usually give the traditional greeting that often unexpectedly provides a "relative" in another location. Kluckhohn and Leighton suggest, "Clans may be thought of

as threads of sentimental linkage which bind together Navajos who are not biologically related, who have not grown up in the same locality, who may indeed never see each other, or may do so but once in a lifetime" (Kluckhohn and Leighton 1974, 112). There is a resurgence of clan identity on Dinétah today as many Navajos try to follow "the corn pollen rule" and reestablish their cultural roots.

Approximately sixty clans exist in the Navajo clan system (Iverson 1990, 29). As with many of the cultural components of the Diné, there is a connection between the clans and the creation story. For example, Changing Woman created the first four clans from the skin of her body. According to *Navajo History,*

> Changing Woman thought that there should be more people, so she created more of them [humans] by rubbing the skin from her breast, from her back and from under both arms. In this way she created the first four clans. Changing Woman rubbed the skin from her breast and formed people who became the Kiiyaa'áanii clan. From the skin rubbed from her back the Honágháahnii clan was formed. From the skin under her right arm the Tó Dích'íi'nii clan was created, and from the skin under her left arm the Hashtł'ishnii clan was made. (Yazzie 1971, 74)

Translations of the first four clan names show their connection with physical traits, personality characteristics, the environment, and animals: Kiiyaa'áanii, also spelled Kinyaa'áanii (Towering House), Honágháahnii (One Walks Around You), Tó Dích'íi'nii (Bitter Water), and Hashtł'ishnii (Mud). Since the Diné permit intermarriage with non-Navajos, new clans evolved and the number of clans increased.

The clan system is grounded on the matrilineage of each clan member and is the foundation of the Navajo family system. The Diné use special names for clan members, depending on whether they are referring to the mother's clan or the father's clan. A child's mother is called *shimá;* her mother's sister, *shimáyázhí;* and her maternal grandmother, *shimásání.* The child's father is called *shizhé'é;* her father's sister; *shibízhí,* and her paternal grandmother, *shinálí* (Lynch 1993, 27). Children may call their mother's sisters' children "sister" and "brother," even though they are not directly related, rather than "cousins," as in white society. The original purpose of clans was to prevent intermarriage among relatives of the same clans. Locke states, "Nowadays the principal importance of clan is that of limiting marriage choices: one may never marry within one's own clan nor that of one's father, although the latter is not considered as incestuous as it once was. The Navajos still look upon incest and the practice of witchcraft as the most repulsive of crimes and marriage within your own clan is thought of as incest" (Locke 1992, 20). Even though not all Navajos know their clans today, traditional Navajos still honor the clan system, especially in regard to the selection of a mate. They indicate their clans by stating who they are "born of" (their mother's clan), "born for" (their father's clan), their maternal grandfather's clan, and their paternal grandfather's clan.

The clan system also established a framework of social order. Kluckhohn and Leighton observe, "The importance of his relatives to the Navajo can scarcely be exaggerated. The worst that one may say of another person is, 'He acts as if he didn't have any relatives.' Conversely, the ideal of behavior often enunciated by headmen is, 'Act as if everybody were related to you'" (Kluckhohn and Leighton 1974, 100). Marilyn Help observed this in her teaching. At the beginning of the school year, many of her students dressed like gang members, in baggy, saggy clothes. She explained to them the significance of the clan system and that in hostile behavior toward another gang, they might actually be hurting a clan "brother" or family member on the other side. Marilyn observed marked improvement in the behavior of her students once they realized the meaningfulness of their clans.

Clan members provide emotional and financial support to one another and often share their material possessions. They actively participate in their clan's ceremonials, celebrations, and other family rituals and events. At a traditional Navajo wedding the bride's family and her clan members supply, prepare, and cook the food that they serve first to the groom's family and guests. Clan members also contribute money and materials for ceremonials when requested by a clan "relative."

Marilyn Help believes in the relevance of the traditional Navajo clan system. She teaches and promotes the use of it with her students, starting with herself.

I am born of Bitter Water Clan and born for Yucca Fruit Strung in a Line Clan. My maternal grandfather's clan is Darkened with the Charcoal Streaked Red Running into the Water Clan and my paternal grandfather's clan is the Black Streaked Wood Clan. Traditional Navajos introduce themselves by stating their clans. Although not all Navajos honor this tradition, there is currently a revival because many schools are stressing the Diné traditional ways and bilingual education. Because of this a lot of our people are becoming aware of the clan system again and are keeping it alive. It is a good tradition, and I am glad it is being revived. My mother is born of Bitter Water Clan and born for Darkened with the Charcoal Streaked Red Running into the Water Clan. My father was born of Yucca Fruit Strung in a Line and born for Black Streaked Wood Clan. My oldest daughter, Shannon, is born of Bitter Water Clan and born for Towering House.

You automatically have a clan from the time that you are born. Your clan tells you that you must not intermarry with the same clan. This is told in the creation story by the Holy People. They intermarried and had monster children who were handicapped. Learn from this teaching. Do not intermarry within your clan. I teach this to my children because I want them to know who they are and where they are coming from.

The Song Connection

The significance of clans in Navajo culture is exemplified in the selection of partners for traditional dances. When women and girls select a dance partner, they ascertain whether or not they are in the same clan. Since dancing has an element of courtship that can lead to marriage, traditional Navajos dance together only if they are not clan relatives.

"Yo'oo' Eidoo-o' Hee Yee"

(A Dance Song)

Background Information

You would use this song at the Enemy-way ceremony, on the first or second night. People really enjoy this one. This is a social dance song. I learned this song from a group of singers called the Whip-poorwill Singers, a dance group that is good. They are the ones that sing it. It is a traditional song that they sang, and I learned it. I have sung this song for my students at school, and they have danced to it. We also have clapped our hands and moved our feet to it, using our gross motor skills. The kids love this song. They don't want to just sit there and sit there and sing. They want to do body movements to it. We do motions to a lot of the songs that I sing to them. This is a song for everybody for entertainment.

Well, you know what? When you begin to learn a song, not everybody will learn a song just like that. My father, the way that he teaches us, says that if the song is meant for a person, that person will be able to just pick it up and learn it the same day. It is like that even with the ceremonies. He said that there is this one medicine man who learned all of these ceremonial songs in five days and he knew the whole ceremonial by just following his grandfather. That is how he learned it.

There are certain songs that I can just pick up even by just listening to it one time. They say that in our traditional way if you learn a song like that it is meant to be. The Holy People want you to know it, so you just pick it up right away. But there are certain songs that if it doesn't want to come to you, then it won't come to you. But there are certain songs that will. You will learn the song in one day or just by listening to it one time and then it is meant for you and that is the way it is.

I think that this is a rather recent song. It doesn't go back for a long time.

Since the traditional way of learning music in Navajo culture is through listening, repetition, and practice, it is common for the Diné to sing and share songs that they hear at the Enemyway ceremony or a Song and Dance Contest. Once a song is heard, it is permissible to sing it and perform it for others. Because these songs are passed on from one person to another through oral tradition, it is often impossible to trace the origin of a song. Many Navajo recordings feature contemporary singers performing the traditional Squaw Dance repertoire as well as more recently composed pieces. A listing of recording artists can be found at the end of this book in the Selected Discography section.

Information about the music

After two introductory drumbeats, Marilyn sings a common introductory vocable pattern, *"Hee yee' yąą' ą',"* on the tonic, or home tone. Then the melody leaps up an octave and falls to the tonic once again for the recurring *"hee yee' yąą' ą'"* vocable pattern. As with numerous other examples of traditional Navajo music, the tonic acts as a magnet. Throughout the song the melody rises and falls, only to return to the home tone with great regularity.

The lyrics of this song consist entirely of vocable patterns. The introductory formula occurs throughout the song as well as at the end of phrases. In addition, a variant of this pattern appears at the very end of the song, *"hee yee' ya wee yąą' ą',"* which signals the dancers that the song is ending.

Although the beat is steady throughout the piece, there are many changing meters due to the mixture of vocable patterns. The underlying feeling is of the beat subdivided into sets of three.

Experiencing the music

Once the listener recognizes and identifies the various vocable patterns and the repetitions of each section, he or she can learn to sing the song. The stately, steady beat of the music invites participants to dance this popular Two-step or, as Marilyn says, the "high-step." After the ladies choose their male partners, the dancers lift their feet and step to the beat in a lively manner. The dancers move clockwise with their partners around the circle in time to the music. The female dancer joins hands or hooks elbows and follows the male partner's lead on which foot to use to begin the dance.

Interlinear Translation and Translation

Since the song "Yo'oo' Eidoo-o' Hee Yee" consists of vocables only, no translation is needed.

Yo'oo' Eidoo-o' Hee Yee

(A Dance Song)

hee   ei hee yee - ee,   yo'   oo' ei - doo   -   o' hee   yee,

yo'   oo' ei doo   -   o' hee   laa,   hee yee'   yaa'   a',

Yo' oo' ei - doo - o   hee yee,   yo' oo' ei - doo   -   o hee   yee,

yo' oo' ei doo   -   o hee laa,   hee yee'   ya wee   yaa'   a'.

Plate 1

Marilyn Help, wearing her traditional Navajo rug dress, biil'éé'. Leggings, kénitsaaí, are wrapped around her lower legs. She is holding a small frame drum. Her turquoise ring, necklace, belt, and pin identify her as the Diné, the Navajo, to the Holy People.

Plate 2
Joni and Shannon (Marilyn Help's daughters), rodeo princesses, at the Gallup Intertribal
Ceremonial.

Plate 3

Marilyn Help and her father, John C. Help, holding the "Pueblo-style" drum that is heard on the accompanying recording.

Plate 4
Mummy Cave Ruin in Canyon del Muerto, Canyon de Chelly, Chinle, Arizona.

Plate 5
Monument Valley, Navajo Nation, Utah. Photo by Marla Geltner.

Plate 6
Rock formation for which the capital of the Navajo Nation is named, Window Rock.

Plate 7

Mountain goat petroglyph in Monument Valley, Navajo Nation, Utah. Photo by Marla Geltner.

Plate 8
A petroglyph of horses running down a deer in Canyon de Chelly, Chinle, Arizona.
Photo by Marla Geltner.

Plate 9
Pictograph of ceremonial dancers, Deligalito Canyon, New Mexico.
Photo by Marla Geltner.

Plate 10
First hogan of First Man and First Woman on Huerfano Mesa, Farmington, New Mexico.
Photo by Marla Geltner.

Plate 11
Overview of Canyon de Chelly, Chinle, Arizona.
Photo by Marla Geltner.

Plate 12

Marilyn Help's paternal grandmother, her *shinálí,* made the Navajo blanket. On the left are stirring sticks made out of greasewood, *ideestsijn.* The metate, *tsé deeshjee',* is the lower grinding stone. The handheld grinder, *mano,* is called *tsé deeshch'iní.* A Navajo hairbrush, *bé'azhóó,* is on the right.

Plate 13
Sheep marked with the brand G, for Marilyn Help's mother, Grace Help.

Plate 14
Angora goat, Monument Valley, Navajo Nation, Utah. Photo by Marla Geltner.

Plate 15
A female earth hogan in Monument Valley, Navajo Nation, Utah. Photo by Marla Geltner.

Plate 16
Spider Rock, Canyon de Chelly, Chinle, Arizona. Photo by Marla Geltner.

Chapter 9

LIVESTOCK

The Song . . .

"Łį́į́ Ch'ééh Háánítóó"
(Looking for a Horse)

One of the most striking and memorable features of the Navajo Nation landscape is the preponderance of sheep, a sight pictured in a multitude of tourist guides. A visitor traveling among the four sacred mountains may see sheep in corrals as well as sauntering casually on the road. Dogs, children, or even young teenagers on mopeds tend them. Sheep, horses, goats, cattle, and even stray dogs provide a breathtaking counterpoint to the backdrop of red rocks. Because of the great variety of animal life that travels freely on the reservation, drivers typically see road signs cautioning visitors to watch for livestock on the highway. (see Plates 13 and 14)

Livestock has long been an integral part of Navajo culture. Past generations of the Diné measured wealth based on the number of animals a Navajo family owned. But this is not necessarily the case today. Marilyn Help suggests that material wealth, such as the kind of house you live in and whether or not it has electricity and running water, as well as the type of truck you drive, is the criterion for measuring the wealth of a contemporary Navajo family. Therefore, although many traditional Navajos still raise livestock, the number of sheep or horses a family owns does not guarantee an elevated status in the community.

Livestock does have a strong cultural link to the traditional Diné way of life. Johnson and Roessel say that the Diné believe that the Holy People gave them the gift of animals, which explains why they value their livetock so much (Roessel and Johnson 1974, 224). Non-Navajo historians attribute the introduction of horses and sheep to the Diné and Pueblo people to the early Spanish settlers in the late seventeenth and early eighteenth centuries. One thing is certain: livestock has been and is an integral part of Navajo culture.

The impact of horses and sheep on the Diné lifestyle was profound. Horses enabled the Diné to travel quickly as they went on forays to recapture their women and children who were stolen in slave raids. They also provided the Navajo with quick transportation to seize sheep and other livestock from their enemies, often in retribution for their crimes. Sheep supplied food, such as mutton for stew, and wool for weaving, a staple in the traditional Navajo woman's life. All family members owned and took care of sheep, especially children. In fact, children learned valuable lessons about family responsibility and commitment by tending their lambs. The Diné gave sheep to the medicine person as payment for ceremonials. Sheep were also slaughtered to provide food for all of the guests who attended rituals (Iverson 1990, 31). Traditional Navajos still use sheep for the same purposes today.

During the eighteenth and first half of the nineteenth century the Navajo livestock population increased dramatically, enabling families to feed themselves and prosper. It was a bitter blow for the Diné when they were forced to give up their livestock and go on the Long Walk to Fort Sumner. Their herds were greatly reduced and in many cases totally destroyed.

After their four years of captivity at Bosque Redondo, the government gave a limited number of animals to the Diné to replenish their herds as part of the 1868 treaty. Because of their successful animal husbandry skills, Navajo livestock increased rapidly by the turn of the century. The Diné had increased their population of sheep and goats from approximately 40,000 in 1868 to over 800,000 (Iverson 1990, 50). This success with livestock led to another problem.

By the end of the nineteenth century the soil in the Navajo Nation was eroding at an alarming rate from animal overgrazing. In the late 1920s and early 1930s erosion on the reservation reached a critical peak. Government officials told the Diné that they must voluntarily reduce their sheep, cattle, horses, and goats. The Navajo countered with a different solution to the soil erosion problem—if they had more land, they would have more grass for their animals to graze. In fact, the U.S. Congress did pass legislation several times in the early part of the twentieth century that increased the Navajo Nation land base. But the problem still existed: there were too many animals and not enough grazing land to feed them.

In addition, the government did not understand the unwritten rules for grazing that the Navajo had honored for decades. A Navajo family who had traditionally used land for grazing had the first rights to it. Locke describes this system: "Farm and range lands are said to 'belong' to the family that has traditionally used it. A man never inherits the use-ownership of his wife's property but he might, conceivably, inherit that of his mother or sisters" (Locke 1992, 18). As a result, when the government suggested restricting and designating land usage, there was great resistance from the Diné. The stage was set for another battle between the Navajo and the government, a crisis that still causes bitter feelings and anger from the Diné whenever they discuss it. It was the time of the livestock reduction plan, implemented by the new Commissioner of Indian Affairs, John Collier.

Although well intentioned (a viewpoint held by historians but not necessarily by the Navajo), Collier was unable to persuade the Diné to voluntarily reduce their livestock. He promised them what he could: more land, better schools, and jobs (Iverson 1990, 63). But he failed to win their trust. The government hoped that the Navajo would willingly reduce their stock once they understood the gravity of the erosion problem on their land. The officials did not effectively communicate their reasons to the Diné, however, especially to Navajo women, who owned many of the sheep (Locke 1992, 445). The government clearly failed to understand the significance of livestock in traditional Navajo culture.

The voluntary stock reduction plan was implemented in 1933–35. Because erosion continued at an alarming rate, an involuntary program was implemented for the next several years; the atrocities began. Stories still circulate regarding the brutal destruction of animals. Locke states, "Agents were sent through the country and thou-

sands of goats were shot and left to rot. Over 3,500 goats were destroyed in Navajo Canyon in a single day. Then thousands of horses were destroyed in the same manner. This wanton destruction of the animals they had raised incensed the Navajos" (Locke 1992, 446). Although these events occurred many decades ago, Marilyn Help still recollects the anger and frustration of her people.

I think my people really got hurt by the livestock reduction program because they are really close to their animals ... the sheep, the horses, and the cows. I understand that when there was an overabundance of them, the government came and took the cattle and the sheep and they just shot them. They threw them into a pit and burned them. They burned the carcasses. Our people cried. My people, they cried. They thought that this act was another Hwééldi, Long Walk. They asked the government, "Why are you doing this to us? What are you doing? You gave the animals for us to use, and now you are turning around and killing our livestock."

The Diné held the position that livestock provided their foundation of economic support. If the Navajo reduced their animal inventory, how would they eat? Where would they get their mutton stew? How could they pay the medicine person for a ceremony? How could they teach their children how to behave properly if they had no sheep to tend (Iverson 1990, 74)? These questions and many others resounded whenever the livestock reduction issue was discussed. Nonetheless, the livestock reduction plan was implemented by the government, forcing the Diné to readjust and reorganize their culture and their lives in order to conform to the ideas of the dominant white society.

Roessel and Johnson criticize the stock reduction program in their book *Navajo Livestock Reduction: A National Disgrace.* They state, "The reduction or elimination of something that is measured in spiritual as well as material value is filled with danger, particularly when those responsible are exclusively concerned with resource management (material) rather than the emotional (spiritual) values" (Roessel and Johnson 1974, 224). Regardless of whether or not it was a battle between materialism and spiritualism, the stock reduction program forced the Diné to find other means of livelihood and to become less dependent on their beloved animals. Marilyn Help is philosophical about it.

I can see both sides of it. There was animal overpopulation, and the grass was ruined. A long time ago the grass around this area was very high, and now there is nothing. It is because of overgrazing. However, the young people now are not as interested as they used to be in raising animals. The older people wanted the land to raise sheep. But now, the younger generation, it seems like they don't want to herd sheep. Therefore, there is a lot less sheepherding now. So, erosion and

livestock management might balance out.

Without a doubt, the livestock reduction program had a powerful impact on traditional Navajo life and culture, the memories of which still echo today.

Although Marilyn Help recognizes the need for balancing livestock ownership with protecting the earth from erosion, she also sees the value of raising animals and believes the benefits are incalculable. She encourages her children to carry on the same cultural tradition. For example, her family could move to a house with running water, but they choose to live in their home in Tolakai so that they can have their livestock on their land near to them. Her choice of housing means that her children can take care of their livestock every day, as she did when she was a young girl.

I learned responsibility when I herded sheep for my grandmother. I was probably about three or four. My grandmother had a lot of sheep. She would separate the little lambs from the rest of the herd. I think there were as many as eighty lambs. I herded them all by myself. I loved those little lambs because they would just be jumping around and bouncing all over the place. They would play around on their own. Sometimes I would scare them. I would run at them, and they would come running together all at once. And then sometimes I would just lie there. They would get really curious, and they would start coming to me and nibbling on my ear. They chewed on my hair, and I would let them do it. This was when I was three or four, probably four because it was before I went to school. I used to just lie there, and they could nibble at me all they wanted to. I would giggle and giggle and just lie there. The lambs did not have individual names because there were so many of them. But I thought each one of them was very special.

We are raising horses and sheep on our land now. I think we have five horses and maybe thirty or forty sheep. We have named some of them but not all of them. We all take care of them, although my dad does the most tending. But we all try to help when we can, and we buy them feed, hay, and grain. We try not to overgraze because I tell my dad that it ruins the grass for the horses and the sheep. I tell him that we have to keep our herd small, rather than having a big herd.

We mark and brand our sheep. I don't have my own marking, so we use my mom's earmark. Her mark is a slash on one side of the ear and a notch that goes in two different directions on the other. We mark their ears, and the first time we do it, there is a lot of blood. In the old days, they used to dip their sheep to protect them from disease. But now we give them shots or put medication on their backs after we shear them. We brand them with the letter G for Grace, my mom's name.

Some of our people have a summer and winter camp for their sheep. We just have our livestock in the same place all year round. My grandmother had three places where she moved her sheep, depending on the time of the year.

When we make mutton stew, we slaughter our own sheep for the meat. We usually butcher a wether, a castrated male sheep, and try to find one of the biggest ones. I know how to slaughter the sheep myself. Traditionally, before you slaughter a sheep, you must talk to it and tell it that it is here for the purpose of supplying food. You say, "I am going to take your life for our food." Then you take some wool from the sheep and throw it into the herd. After you do this, the sheep knows that its life is going to be taken.

The thing about the sheep is that you use every bit of it. You do not throw any of it away. Every bit of it has to be used, even the tripe, the stomach. You just wash it really well and clean it really well and then afterward you cook it with corn. I think the intestines are the best part of a lamb to eat. After you clean it really well, then you take the stomach lining, it's like a fat, and you wrap it with the intestine round and round and put it on the grill. The liver and the ribs are good, too. My kids also like the intestine because when it's cooked right, it's kind of crunchy and they like to chew it.

We also like mutton stew. The traditional recipe for mutton stew is to cook just the meat by itself. But once we got to know potatoes, we cooked them with the mutton. Now people make it real fancy and use vegetables like carrots and celery with the meat. You can also use blue corn meal and put it into the stew. It makes those little dumplings, and the older people really like that.

There are traditional songs that may be sung to the sheep. When you go to a Hózhǫ́ǫ́jí, you can sing those songs. They call them the *dibé biyiin*. My dad knows these songs; the sheep and the horse songs, too.

Taking care of livestock is very important when you raise kids. It teaches them to be responsible for their animals. I want my children to value sheep and sheepherding. That's why I have livestock where I live. Because otherwise I probably would have moved them to a more modern home. But I do not want to move because I want them to know the same values that I was brought up with. I want them to appreciate these values as they get older. If they know at least a little bit of the Diné way, then they can share that with their own children. I really stress this idea to them now.

In addition to her sheep, Marilyn loves horses. She notes that horses are very popular in contemporary Navajo culture, especially for their use in rodeos. She enthusiastically recounts her rodeo experiences and her family's affection for horses:

When I was young, I used to ride in the rodeo. My specialties were barrel racing, goat tying, and sometimes pole bending. It was so much fun. I just used to love to do that. My children also enjoy riding, even my dad. Since my dad was raised with livestock, that's all he wants to do. He just wants to keep on riding when he's outside doing livestock work all of the time. All of his brothers are like that, too. They do a lot of riding.

Marilyn's daughters also ride their horses in parades and competitions for beauty contests. Lyle, Marilyn's oldest son, rides junior bulls in the rodeo and hopes to qualify for the regular ranked bulls event. Her youngest son, Shane, enjoys "woolly riding," or sheep riding.

As Marilyn describes above, traditional Navajo families still raise livestock today. She notes that in many areas on the Navajo Nation, the grazing rules of the past still reign. Nonetheless, the Diné have had to build many more fences on the reservation today than in the past. These inevitably restrict and ignore traditional grazing rights.

Traditional Navajos still believe that livestock are a gift from the Holy People. Like Marilyn, they encourage their children to raise sheep and goats and ride horses so that they continue to celebrate their culture in time-honored ways.

The Song Connection

Since the Diné value livestock so much, animals are mentioned frequently in the lyrics of Navajo songs. Marilyn and her father wrote the song "Łį́į́ Ch'ééh Háánítóó," which describes someone who is "trying to look for horses" in a halfhearted way. They feel that this song presents a cultural value about work ethics: Don't be lazy.

"Łį́į́ Ch'ééh Háánítóó"
(Looking for a Horse)

Background Information

I created this song with the help of my dad. With the way we were putting our words together, it just came together by itself. It is a social song. Kids can learn it and perform some sort of a rhythm dance or a game to it, like moving their arms and legs or passing something around to keep the rhythm. You can also dance to it and sing it in a Song and Dance Contest. If you wanted to sing it during the Enemyway singing, you would do it for the first night or second night. There are different song types that they sing, and you can go ahead and use it during one of those times, whichever one has the right rhythm.

This song is talking about looking for a horse. It is like a teaching. It says to get up and look for your horse as early as you can because the person in the song is getting a little lazy. That is why he lost his horse. He is standing where there is a pointed rock and trying to look around for his horse. It is like a moral teaching. I think that horses are really valued in our way because we have sacred songs for them. "Looking for a Horse" is a social song. The sacred songs about horses are sung in the Beautyway, or Hózhǫ́ǫ́jí.

Marilyn and her father, John C. Help, composed this song during the recording session for this project. It was a joyous experience to see them singing together, bantering back and forth as Marilyn tried out different melodies and phrases for the song. After several attempts, Marilyn sang a version of the song that they both liked.

Information about the music

"Looking for a Horse" illustrates several musical characteristics that are common in traditional Navajo music (McAllester and Mitchell 1983, 606). The melody uses only four notes of the scale: the tonic, third, fifth, and sixth. When the tonic, third, and fifth scale degrees interweave sequentially, the notes outline the tonic chord.

There are three vocable patterns in "Looking for a Horse." The first is the introductory formula, *"hee nee' yąą' ą',"* which is followed by a longer vocable sequence, *"Ei nee yaa hee yoo'oo, ei nee yaa hee yoo'oo, ei nee yaa hee yoo, hee ya hee nee ya'."* This second vocable pattern repeats frequently in the song and functions as a refrain that appears before and after each new section of the tune that has a translatable Navajo text. The third vocable pattern, *"hee ya hee nee ya',"* occurs as the last part of the second vocable formula as well as the cadential phrase that appears at the end of the translatable word sections.

Although Marilyn refers to this song as a "high-step" or "Two-step" song, it does fit the criteria that McAllester outlines for a Circle Dance. The underlying beat sub-divides into threes. In addition, the vocables *"hee nee ya'"* occur at the end of each sec-tion. "Looking for a Horse" also has fre-quent meter changes that accommodate the text.

Experiencing the music

Marilyn suggests that "Looking for a Horse" is an excellent song to use for feeling the beat of the music by moving various body parts, such as clapping or patting the thighs, to the pulse of the music. These movement activities act as a motivator and warm-up activity before learning the dance that accompanies the song. As in a Squaw Dance, females choose male partners and join hands or hook elbows as they face clockwise in a circle and perform the Two-step or, as Marilyn prefers to call it, the "high-step" dance. Partners lift their feet higher than they would in a normal walking movement as they step to the beat in a lively manner. The partners match their steps with each other by starting the dance with the same foot, which may be either the right or the left one. Since Marilyn classifies this song as part of the contemporary Squaw Dance reper-toire, she requests that it only be performed between the first thunder of spring and the first frost of winter in order to honor the time strictures of the Enemyway ceremony.

Interlinear Translation

Łį́į́	(horse)
ch' ééh	(trying)
háánítóó	(to search or to look)
T'áá	(just)
ni	(you)
nił	(with)
hóyéego	(laziness)
biniinaa	(that is why)
Ałt'ą̨	(now)
naaghái	(over close by)
tsé	(rock)
dééz'áhódóó	(from pointing out rock)
náhénoó*	(rotating in one place; turning around in one place)

*Note: náhénoó is a shortened word, a contraction, for náheenaał.

Translation

Łį́į́ ch'ééh háánítóó.	You are trying to look for a horse.
T'áá ni nił hóyéego biniinaa.	Because you are lazy, that is why.
Ałt'ą̨ naaghái tsé dééz'áhódóó náhénoó (náheenaał).	That is why you are now standing at the rock point turning around.

Łį́į́ Ch'ééh Háánítóó

(Looking for a Horse)

Chapter 10

HOGANS

The Song . . .

"Kiizh"
(Spot)

To the novice, a hogan is a curious sight that at first glance may seem nothing more than a traditional dwelling place of the Navajo. The hogan, however, is a cultural icon that symbolizes the traditional Navajo way of life and the teachings of the Holy People. (see Plate 15)

As with many other components of Navajo culture, the Diné creation story describes the origin of the first hogan. According to Yazzie, Talking God gave First Man and First Woman instructions on how to build a hogan.

The people constructed a hogan of five logs, following Talking God's instruc-tions. The first two logs came from east and west, the next two from south and north, and the fifth from the north-east. In blessing the hogan, they blessed only four sides. Today only four sides of a hogan are blessed. On the roof, where they placed the end of the east log, they put white shell; under the south log, turquoise; under the west log, abalone; under the north log, obsidian, and under the fifth log, jewels from all directions. Where the logs came together at the roof top, they tied feathers of different birds. The tips of the logs are thought to be the eyes of the hogan.

(Yazzie 1971, 19)

Medicine persons bless newly constructed hogans with corn pollen and prayers according to the teachings of the Holy People. Locke supports this idea: "Once completed, the new hogan is consecrated with a Blessing Way rite whereby the Holy People are asked to 'let this place be happy'" (Locke 1992, 15).

Although the Navajo nation is dotted with homes of many sizes and shapes, hogans are still essential to the traditional Navajo way of life. A hogan provides the site for ceremonies and may be male or female. The male hogan design is four logs forked together and covered with earth. Male hogans are the oldest style and are rarely seen today. The female hogan is the more familiar to cultural outsiders. Made out of wood, it has six or eight sides and is circular in design. The doors of both male and female hogans face the east, to honor Father Sun and to receive blessings from the Holy People. In past generations a hogan was abandoned if a person died in it. A hole was punched out in the evil, or north, side, and the body was removed (Kluckhohn and Leighton 1974, 89).

Some Navajos choose to live in hogans as their main dwelling place. Hogans are also used for storage and work areas when not in use for ceremonies. Due to their clever design and construction, hogans are cool in the summer and warm in the winter. Another characteristic of the hogan is the opening at its top that allows smoke from the fire or wood-burning stove to escape. Some hogans have windows and screen doors that allow the outside air to circulate. And there are even hogans that sport television sets inside with satellite dishes right outside the door. A few hogans have been designated especially for tourist viewing, such as the one at the Canyon de Chelly visitor station outside of Chinle, Arizona. It illustrates the usual design but is not furnished. In addition, hogan bed-and-breakfasts are available for those who want to experience traditional Navajo customs by eating native foods and sleeping on a mattress on the dirt floor.

Marilyn describes the traditional Navajo hogan in detail, including the symbolism and meaning behind the four directions represented in the structure.

The male hogan is the stick-forked structure, and the female hogan is the round design. A door on a hogan always faces east because all good things rise with the sun. Everything good comes in with the sunshine. The sun is the father. We always address the sun as the father when we pray. The first thing we say is Mother Earth and Father Sky, which would be the sun, the sun himself. And so we believe that we need to teach our children early in the morning because Father Sun is very strict. The morning is the time to teach young children the values that you want them to know.

The four directions represented in the hogan explain our Diné philosophy of learning and our traditional way of life. The hogan has the East, the South, the West, and the North. From the east side we have birth, from the south side we have the child, a young girl or a young boy, from the west side we have the young woman or the young man, and finally from the north we have the elderly woman and the elderly man. Finally you go back to old age again at the end, and that's what they call "going back into old age."

Then at the same time the East has spring, the South has summer, the West has fall, and the North has winter. And so that's how the seasons fit in with the four directions in the hogan.

In addition, there is thinking to the east and the planning of things to the south. To the west we have life, and to the north we have love, hope, and charity. All these things work together. Each direction in the hogan is represented by the different types of cultural things that the Diné have. And so the hogan is a very, very special place.

I always teach my students that we need to respect Mother Earth because she gives life to all living things. There's a purpose for everything, even down to the smallest ant. When you talk about an ant, some children like to run over and kick an anthill or whatever. But I tell my students that it is not nice to go and run over there to kick somebody's house because that is the ant's home. We need to have respect, even down to the smallest creature. I always give examples and say that what if there was a big giant who threw a big rock on your house or stepped on your home? If that happened, you probably would not like

it, so let's have some respect for our homes because that's where all of the good things are.

We always have our fire in the middle of the hogan. That goes back to the main natural laws of water, air, Mother Earth, and fire. We have respect for all four of them. These are the essential natural elements. They are the sacred life givers for us as human beings. We depend on them and need to respect them. When we throw wood in the fire to feed it, we say a prayer and say thank you to the fire for cooking our food. We also thank the water for being a life giver to always moisten the earth and even to moisten us because we have to have water all of the time.

So these are the things that the hogan shows us. The hogan and these ideas were given to us by the Holy People. They showed us how to build a hogan, and that is why we build them accordingly. The Holy People instructed our people to have a blessing every time we move into a new hogan. You touch the east side with corn pollen and also the south, west, and north. That is how a hogan is usually blessed. A medicine man can do it or, if you have a summer camp somewhere, you can do it yourself, too. You just say your prayers with it and do your own ceremony, a small ceremony to put the corn pollen on it.

Colors are also associated with the hogan. To the east we have white, the white shell, to the south we have turquoise, to the west we have yellow, and to the north we have black.

A long time ago they say that only the male hogan was used for ceremonies, but now I notice that both the male and female hogans are being used. When we have a drought, they use the male hogan in order to do the ceremony to bring the rain. That was done last year. But other ceremonies, like the Kinaaldá, can be performed in a female hogan.

My family slept in a hogan when we were growing up. My sisters and brothers and I did not have a bed. We slept under a table or wherever else we could find a spot. My mom and dad slept on the bed, probably with the baby, but the rest of us would sleep on the floor, side by side. And there were a lot of us in the hogan, too. But my sisters and I would not sleep next to our brothers; they would sleep on the other side.

As Marilyn so aptly describes it, the hogan is a very special place for the Diné. Hogans supply shelter as well as spiritual comfort and healing. They act as a powerful cultural symbol for the Navajo. One can well imagine how close and connected a family is to one another when they live in such close quarters, sharing the same space, cultural values, and communion with the Holy People.

The Song Connection

Songs about hogans are not included in this text because of their sacredness. Although there are social songs that mention hogans, Marilyn chose instead to sing about a pet dog, a typical beloved inhabitant that often resides outside the family hogan.

"Kiizh"
(Spot)

Background Information

My preschoolers like to sing this song all the time. I think the children learned it from the tape that Dollie Yazzie made [*Navajo Music for Class-room Enrichment*]. The kids act out the motions to the song with hand movements to show the different body parts of the dog. They enjoy it, too.

I had a pet dog when I was growing up. I called her Patty. I had another special dog, too; we called her Nuffy. Her nickname was Nuff. They were my two special dogs. Patty was like a cocker spaniel, but Nuffy was a small dog, almost like a poodle. Nuffy was a fuzzy dog, really nice and cute and always jumping around. They didn't herd sheep. They were just dogs that took care of the home. They didn't get to sleep in the hogan at night. My mom and dad wouldn't let them in. I wanted them to come in, but my parents said no.

"Spot" is a popular song that Navajo children enjoy. Several of the phrases describe the body parts of "Kiizh" and how they move. Children try to imitate these humorous antics as they sing the song. Another variant of " Spot" is in the book *Navajo Music for Classroom Enrichment*, edited by Dollie Yazzie. The version of the song that appears in this book is Marilyn's own interpretation of the song and her adaptation of the movements that accompany the lyrics.

Information about the music

The melody of "Spot" is loosely based on two Anglo-American tunes: "Hush, Little Baby" and "My Dog Wags." Appendix D illustrates the English translation and corresponding movements of this funny song about a dog. With the exception of the fourth phrase in the melody line, excluding the vocable introduction, the melodies are very similar. It is interesting that a vocable pattern occurs at the beginning of the song that outlines fragments of the melody. Perhaps the Diné add these vocables to make the song more Navajo-like. The majority of notes in the song are quarter and eighths, with a smattering of dotted quarter and eighth note patterns. Although chords could be easily played as an accompaniment to this song, Marilyn prefers the single sound of the drumbeat for the background.

Experiencing the music

The vocable pattern in this song is the easiest part to learn. It occurs at the beginning, middle, and end of the song, with the exception of the last coda phrase. Since each of the other phrases of the music uses different Navajo words, they are challenging to master. Nonetheless, with numerous repetitions, the whole song can be sung with the appropriate corresponding movements, found in Appendix D.

Interlinear Translation

Shí	(mine alone)
shilééchąą'í	(my dog)
éí	(that one)
Kiizh	(spotted)
wólyé	(is called)
T'áá	(just)
akwíí	(every)
jíí	(day)
shíkéé'	(behind me)
naaldloosh	(it goes)
Bíjáá'	(its ears)
nei	(around)
diłdiłgóó	(flops)
bítséé'	(its tail)
nei	(around)
diłtas	(wags)
T'áá	(just)
akwííjíí	(every day)
bibid	(its stomach)
neishood	(drags)

Translation

Shí shilééchąą'í éí Kiizh wólyé.　　My dog's name is Spot.

T'áá akwííjįį shíkéé' naaldloosh.　　Every day he follows me around.

Bíjáá' nei diłdiłgóó bítséé' nei diłtas.　　He flops his ears; he wags his tail.

T'áá akwííjįį bibid neishood.　　Every day he drags his belly around.

Kiizh
(Spot)

ei nee yoo' o. Shí shi - lee - chąą' - í eí Kiizh wól - yé,

T'aá akwíí - jíí shí - keé' naald - loosh, Bi - jąą' nei dił - dił - góó bí -

D.S. al Coda 𝄋

tseé' nei dił - tas, T'aá akwíí - jíí bi - bid nei - shood,

Ⓕ *Coda*

T'aá akwíí - jíí shi - keé' naald - loosh.

Chapter 11

TRADITIONS AND CUSTOMS

The Song . . .

"We Yaa Naa"
(Apache Love Song)

Traditional Navajo culture provides a wealth of household property that connects the generations of the Diné. Among these are Navajo rugs, jewelry, baskets, cradle boards, grinding stones, and clothing. These material goods have a long history of production and usage that stays alive from one family to the next through oral tradition. An examination of each one illustrates the Navajo idea of beauty, hózhǫ́. Whether a pictorial rug or an exquisite squash blossom necklace, the Diné weave and design material goods that exemplify the beauty of their world. Roessel says, "Navajo life and culture is intertwined with the belief in the significance of harmony and the necessity for beauty. Navajo crafts provide a means for this relationship to be expressed, revealed, and continued" (R. Roessel 1983, 601). Reflecting this sense of beauty, balance, and harmony, rugs and jewelry are perhaps the best-known art products made by the Diné.

Navajo weavers have a national and international reputation for their superior products. They command up to many thousands of dollars for their rugs, which range in design from traditional motifs and colors to contemporary pictures in a kaleidoscope of neon hues. Distinctive weavers are known for their designs in different areas of the Navajo Nation. For example, Locke says that there are thirteen weaving locations, including the Two Gray Hill region, known for their geometric patterns in black, white, gray, and brown, and the Shiprock area, recognized for their Yeibichai designs (pictorial representations of the Holy People) (Locke 1992, 38). As with the many variants of rug designs, there are also several theories that explain the development of Navajo weaving.

Diné weavers credit Spider Woman, one of the Navajo's sacred deities, for their gift of the loom. Gladys Reichard describes this event in her book *Spider Woman: A Story of Navajo Weavers and Chanters:*

> Spider Woman instructed the Navajo women how to weave on a loom which Spider Man told them how to make. The crosspoles were made of sky and earth cords, the warp sticks of sun rays, the healds of rock crystal and sheet lightning. The batten was a sun halo, white shell made the comb. There were four spindles: one a stick of zigzag lightning with a whorl of cannel coal; one a stick of flash lightning with a whorl of turquoise; a third had a stick of sheet lightning with a whorl of abalone; a rain streamer formed the stick of the fourth, and its whorl was white shell (Navajo legend).(Reichard 1968, title page) (see Plate 16)

Some say that Spider Woman lives on the top of Spider Rock in Canyon de Chelly. She is very much alive in the hearts of the Diné—a whole genre of songs is sung especially to her. This music is sacred to Navajos: they perform it only during times they deem appropriate. McAllester and Mitchell write, "There are other kinds of songs, such as weaving songs, that 'have a story,' the origins of which go back to mythical accounts; these too are sacred and reserved for specific occasions" (McAllester and Mitchell 1983, 605). Spider Woman's presence is figuratively seen in traditional and contemporary Navajo rugs. She taught Navajo weavers that they must always weave a "spirit path" in their designs. They intentionally pull one thread to the edge of the blanket, creating an outlet "so the spirit of the weaver will not be imprisoned by its beauty" (Duncan 1996, 29). Locke suggests another explanation for the "spirit path":

> In acknowledgment of their debt to Spider Woman, one of the Holy People of Navajo mythology, Navajo weavers always left a hole in the center of each blanket, like that of a spider's web, until the traders in the early part of this century refused to buy such blankets. Most Navajo weavers still acknowledge the debt by leaving a "spirit outlet" in the design. The spirit outlet usually takes the form of a thin line made from the center of the blanket to the edge, and also serves, Navajo weavers believe, to prevent "blanket sickness." (Locke 1992, 34)

According to Locke, Spider Woman will spin webs in the weaver's mind, causing incoherent thoughts, or "blanket sickness," if the spirit outlet is omitted in the design (ibid., 34).

Although the Diné believe that they learned their weaving from Spider Woman, most non-Navajo historians have concluded that the Pueblos taught the Navajo how to weave. They propose that the Diné learned the basic concept of weaving from them and then made their own adaptations in style and design, which are now quite sophisticated and intricate. Roessel offers another explanation. She says that the Navajo may have learned weaving from their Athabaskan ancestors in the North (R. Roessel 1983, 592). Regardless of which origin theory is correct, the fact remains that Navajo weavers and their rugs have been in great demand since the late eighteenth century. Diné women were often the target of slave raids because of their weaving mastery. And from the late nineteenth century, reservation traders have coveted Navajo rugs for their customers in the East.

Numerous pictures exist from post-Fort Sumner days to the present, depicting the Navajo weaver. She usually poses in front of an enormous, handmade loom built outside her hogan. Dressed in traditional regalia, her face shows great serenity and dignity as she painstakingly weaves her rug design. These pictures reflect the power of the Navajo woman, who in addition to creating a product of great beauty provides a significant source of income for her family.

Silversmithing is another craft that demonstrates the Navajo spirit of loveliness, harmony, and balance. Diné men and women make spectacular silver jewelry, which includes award-winning concha belts, earrings, necklaces, bracelets, bow guards, rings, and button covers. Jewelers often inlay their silver with gems such as turquoise, coral, mother-of-pearl, lapis, and spiny oyster. Traditional Diné wear turquoise daily because it acts as a protector against harm, and they did so even before the arrival of silversmithing because of the precedent set by Turquoise Woman, who dressed in turquoise. It is common to see Navajo elders, men and women alike, dressed in a great deal of exquisite turquoise jewelry. Their attire exemplifies the phrase "more is best."

The history of Navajo silversmithing is unclear. Were Navajos practicing the art before their Fort Sumner captivity? Or did they learn the art of silversmithing there? If they did know silversmithing before their incarceration at Bosque Redondo, who taught them? Did they learn their skills from the Mexicans or from other Native Americans? Although no consensus exists, most historians agree that silversmithing is a relatively recent art form of the Navajo.

In addition to rugs and jewelry, the traditional Navajo wedding basket is a cultural artifact in frequent demand on the reservation. The Diné use these baskets for a number of different rituals. They serve many functions in ceremonies, such as a container for cornmeal or water, a drum, and a dance prop. Navajos and non-Navajos alike call them "Navajo wedding baskets" because of their use in the Navajo wedding ceremony. The bride and groom eat cornmeal or mush from the wedding basket. Other Native American nations, such as the Utes, often make them, and these baskets command a high price at the trading post (Locke 1990, 44). Roessel describes their popularity:

> The traditional need to use Navajo wedding baskets has always been so great that there is a lively trade in used baskets with the trading posts. A Navajo who is going to have a "sing" (ceremony) will go to a trading post and purchase one or more baskets as required. Upon the completion of the "sing" the baskets usually are sold back to the trading post. The same basket may be sold and resold as many as 30 or 40 times a year. (R. Roessel 1983, 602)

The Navajo wedding basket design represents many of the traditional Diné symbols. For example, the colors and patterns portray Mother Earth and Father Sky as well

Figure 10

A Navajo cradle board, in the center, has a condor feather attached to it. The feather was a gift from a friend. Other artifacts include a doll dressed in a "squaw dress" that was made especially for Marilyn Help, a Navajo rug with a "storm pattern" design, stirring sticks, a spindle used for rug weaving (it brings blessings), and corn hanging on the wall, which also brings blessings.

as the rainbow, black clouds, sacred mountains, the lifeline, and the place of emergence.

Cradle boards are yet another traditional artifact of Navajo material culture that connects the generations. Designed to hold infants, they provide protection for the newborn child as the family transports the cradle board during daily activities. As with the Navajo wedding basket, each part of the cradle board represents an aspect of traditional Diné life. For example, the wooden arch that extends from both sides of the cradle board acts as a protector for the baby's head; it also symbolizes the rainbow. This is one of the most potent protective motifs in Navajo graphic art. (see Figure 10)

Traditional Diné women also have grinding stones. Although they are rarely used except for ceremonial functions, such as the Kinaaldá (see chapter 6), they are still valued. Hairbrushes made from greasewood and stirring sticks used in making the cake for the Kinaaldá are other objects of great significance, since they represent a ceremony that is a special blessing for a maturing girl.

Contemporary Navajo women occasionally wear their traditional clothing, the oldest of which is the rug or blanket dress, biil. It is usually handmade by a weaver who creates a red blanket with a black geometric design. In addition to a turquoise necklace, bracelets, and rings, a Navajo woman typically wears a concha belt around her waist. The rug dress is sleeveless and slides easily over the woman's head. Leggings, or kénitsaaí, are wrapped around her legs. She wears leather moccasins on her feet. In addition, the woman wears her hair in a Navajo knot, or tsiiyéél. To create

this traditional hairstyle, the woman pulls back her hair and literally ties it in a knot behind her neck, after which she attaches long strands of white yarn to it. The yarn, shábitł'óól, represents the sun rays. (see Figure 11)

Another popular traditional outfit for Navajo women is a calico skirt and velour shirt. Although some writers suggest that this outfit is an imitation of the clothing of officers' wives at Fort Sumner, others strongly disagree. They suggest that Navajo women copied the dress of schoolteachers and missionaries they met when they returned to live among their four sacred mountains at the end of the nineteenth century.

Marilyn Help owns, uses, and wears many of the traditional artifacts of Navajo culture. She shares her own personal experiences and anecdotes about them.

> I weave rugs. I have not done it lately, but I do know how to weave. When the shearing season comes around again, I want to teach my daughters, Shannon and Joni, how to weave. I will probably put up a loom for them because I want for them to continue the tradition. Both my grandmothers and my mother were weavers. My mother used to weave the Yeibichai design. I only have one rug left. My paternal grandmother wove half of it, and I did the other half.
>
> When you weave, you can set up your loom on either the outside or the inside of your home. In the old days, if

Figure 11
Marilyn Help models her traditional hair-style, a Navajo knot, or tsiiyééł. The yarn represents the rays of sunshine, shábitł'óól.

the loom was outdoors, it was in a place where everything was already set up. Your poles were in the ground, and all you had to do was put up your things. At night you would cover up your weaving and then just start again the next day. I had the more modern type of loom where you could set it up any-where and carry it around wherever you wanted to go.

According to Spider Woman, you have to leave a certain part of the weaving imperfect because if you get stuck in one place, you must find a way out. You cannot just close your mind and say this is where I am going to

stop. You have to open your mind further to broaden your thinking.

I used a cradle board for each of my children that I still have today. Some people attach a squirrel's tail to the cradle board for protection because if a baby falls, you don't want anything bad to happen to the child. When the child is a toddler and falls from a high place like a bed or something, you say the name "squirrel" in Navajo and blow outward with your breath and hope the energies will protect your child from harm. Our people do that because they know that the squirrel is an animal that runs around and falls and jumps all of the time and then recovers and takes off again. We want our children to be like that, too.

My paternal grandmother wore her traditional clothes, necklace, earrings, and bracelet all of the time. She always had her Navajo knot, tsiiyééł, in her hair. And she never, ever, ever took her Navajo knot down. Even when she slept at night, she had her Navajo tsiiyééł. I have tried that, but I can't sleep with my Navajo bun at night. My grandmother only took her hair down when she washed it. She would wash it with a yucca plant. Her hair was very long, down by her legs almost. My grand-mother told me that I should never cut my hair. But when I was a little girl and went to boarding school, they cut it there anyway.

Traditional Navajos wear their hair long. The darker part of your hair is the male, and the ends are the female. But after you tie your hair together in a knot, it represents all of the good things of life. All of your possessions, your clothes, your rugs, your saddles, your bracelets, your jewelry, your vehicle, your horses, and your animals. That's what we call *yódí attas'éí*. That's what you have tied in your knot when you fix your knot. And then when you tie it with white yarn, the yarn represents the sunshine. Each strand is a sunbeam.

I like to wear my traditional clothes, my *tsiitł'óól*. My grandmother told me to always wear a necklace, even a single strand of turquoise, because it will protect me from anything. She said, "These are your protectors. You should always wear something like that." That's why you see Navajo elders with earrings and turquoise.

The material culture of the Navajo—rugs, silver jewelry, baskets, grinding stones, hairbrushes, cornmeal stirrers, and clothing—is vibrantly alive on the reservation. Although many of these artifacts are available for purchase, the astute buyer understands that in many instances they represent special gifts from the Holy People and treats them accordingly.

The Song Connection

Just as many of the traditions and customs honored by the Diné have been influenced by other cultures, so has Navajo music. One of Marilyn's favorite melodies is "Apache Love Song," music that is also sung by the Apache.

"We Yaa Naa"
(Apache Love Song)

Background Information

I learned this song from a friend. Her name was Elva Benson. She passed away about fourteen years ago. She was a real special friend. I am glad that I learned it because now she is not around to sing it. I believe that they call this "Greasewood Song," too, or "Apache Love Song." People often ask me to sing this song when I entertain. I usually include it because it is a social song. It shows respect for the Apache people. You can do a dance with it, too. I have my students make up body movements for it to feel the rhythm and the beat. Although there is not a traditional dance that goes with it, you can do the "high-stepping" one with it.

The Apache and Navajo share several

cultural commonalities. Linguists trace both of their languages to the Athabaskan-speaking people in Alaska and northwestern Canada. This linguistic connection supports the theory that the Apache and Navajo are closely related and migrated to the Southwest together. Their division into two different groups occurred sometime after their arrival in the area. Iverson concurs with this analysis. He states, "Of the many Indian tribes now living in the Southwest, only the Apaches are related linguistically to the Navajos. Therefore, linguists argue that the Apaches and the Navajos were once a single group and probably did not separate until after they had come to their present location. In fact, the Navajos' name is a shortened form of the original Spanish name for them, Apaches de Nabajó (Apaches of the Nabajó)" (Iverson 1990, 18). In addition to their linguistic similarities, they also share a part of the same history.

Both the Apache and Navajo were the target of Brigadier General James Carleton's plan to remove American Indians from their homelands to enable settlers from the eastern United States to explore and settle the Southwest. They were forced to live in the Bosque Redondo during their incarceration at Fort Sumner in the 1860s. Although the Apaches fled from their captivity and so were interned a shorter time at Fort Sumner than the Navajos, they also endured suffering and humiliation.

Besides their linguistic and historical commonalities, McAllester states that there are similarities in their music. In his work

Indian Music in the Southwest, he outlines the following musical characteristics that he finds in Apache, Navajo, and Pueblo music:

1. Almost entirely vocal
2. Musical instruments used as accompaniment (drums, rasps, rattles)
3. Unison singing (rarely part singing)
4. Songs—performed in vigorous manner
5. Melody usually descending to rest on "tonic"
6. Meter—usually duple
7. Texts—long sections of vocables
8. Group singing
9. Religious in nature (McAllester 1961, 1–15)

"Apache Love Song" clearly illustrates many of these musical traits.

Information about the music

Even though the entire song consists of vocables, a distinctive and recognizable vocable pattern (*hee yoo hee' nee ya',*) occurs at the ends of phrases that sets off the other sections. After four introductory beats of the drum, the melodic vocables begin and are continuous until the ending.

Like Navajo music, the most common note values are quarter and eighth notes. In fact, the song contains no other note values except these. And with one exception, the meter projects a duple feeling throughout the tune.

"Apache Love Song" supports McAllester's melodic analysis of southwestern Ameican Indian music. As he points out, the melody descends to rest on the tonic, or home tone.

Experiencing the music

Because of the repetitive vocable patterns, "Apache Love Song" is easy to learn. A Two-step may be performed with this song. After the females choose their partners, each couple either joins hands in a "skating" position, hooks elbows, or the female rests her forearm on the male's forearm. The couple moves forward in a clockwise circle, moving their feet in a sprightly manner. The female partner follows the male's lead as to which foot to begin the dance. They move around the circle in coordinated style.

If the song is sung alone, it may be sung anytime during the year. However, if the Two-step Dance is performed with the song, it should be performed only during the springtime, summer, or early fall to respect the Enemyway ceremony.

Interlinear Translation and Translation

Since the song "We Yaa Naa" consists of vocables only, no interlinear translation or translation is needed.

We Yaa Naa
(Apache Love Song)

We yaa naa, we yaa naa ei yoo' o o,

we yaa naa, we yaa naa ei yoo' o o, we yaa naa, we yaa naa ei yoo' o o,

we yaa naa ei yaa ei yoo' o, hee yoo hee' nee ya',

We yaa naa, we yaa naa ei yoo' o o, we yaa naa, we yaa naa ei yoo' o o,

we yaa naa, we yaa naa ei yoo' o o, we yaa naa ei yaa ei yoo' o,

hee yoo hee' nee ya', oh we yaa naa, oh we yaa naa ei

yoo' o, hee' nee ya', oh we yaa naa, oh we yaa naa ei yoo' o,

we yaa naa ei yaa ei yoo' o, hee yoo hee' nee ya'.

Chapter 12

CONTEMPORARY LIFE

The Song . . .

"Go, My Son"

Navajo culture is not static; it is vibrant, alive, and changing. Although many of the Diné follow the traditional way of life, they are also receptive to new ideas and lifestyles from the surrounding society. They try to balance both worlds effectively. The Diné debate and discuss issues such as gambling, gangs, and drug, alcohol, and child abuse as frequently in the Navajo Nation as anywhere else in America. Navajo children and adults dress in Western-style clothes, eat fast food, rent videos, watch television, view sports, and attend special events just as other Americans do. As has been the case for centuries, the Diné adapt and adjust to new ideas while maintaining their own identity.

Marilyn Help and her family successfully demonstrate how it is possible to balance the past with the present. Marilyn's description of their daily lives illustrates how they juxtapose and accommodate the old with the new.

In the morning I wake up at five o'clock and put water on the stove to warm it up for my kids so that they can wash themselves comfortably. I have to build a fire so that our house will be nice and warm when they arise. My children have to bring in wood or coal the night before so that it's ready for me to use in the morning for the fire.

Sometimes in the winter I have to get up to build the fire during the night so that it will not get too cold inside.

I get ready first. And then I get the older ones up, Shannon and Lyle, so that they can go and help my dad feed the horses. I tell my children to get up early because the Holy People are out there in the morning. I say, "Go out there and talk, talk to the Holy People. This will help you, even though it may be cold outside. You need to talk to the Holy People so that you will have a strong mind and heart. Get out there and run! Start feeding the animals because you will be blessed." I keep telling my children that. Shannon and Lyle do it. But my younger children are spoiled, Joni, Warren, and Shane. They do not go outside; they sleep. They are really hard to get awake in the morning. And when I tell my youngest son, Shane, to get up, he says, "No," and goes back to sleep again. I am after them the whole time to get up and get ready for school. Then when we are finally ready to go, Shane does not have his shoes on, and we all have to run around and find them.

I have to leave at seven o'clock to get them all to school by seven-thirty. They all ride with me, and I take them to school. I would like for the older two to ride the school bus, but they don't want to because the bus is packed full and they have to squeeze in. They also think that everybody is looking at them. Shannon and Lyle try to eat breakfast at home, but the other children eat at school.

Sometimes I cannot fix their evening meal because I have to stay late at the school where I teach. They all take the bus home. Then Shannon fixes their food for them. My dad cooks for them, too, and they like that.

We are also very busy on weekends. My children are involved with sports. We have to get up early so that they can compete in cross-country meets. We would have to be there by seven o'clock. So, I have to get up at five o'clock as usual. I fix them their "noodles" that the coach makes them eat for their running diet. Then we dash off to the recreation center so they can take their bus to the track meet. After that I hurry home to cook breakfast for my other kids, and then we all go to the races to watch them compete. We watch them win. They win all of the time because they are good runners. Now they participate in basketball, so we go to the basketball games, too.

Each one of my children has different interests. Shannon loves to ride and train horses. She is not really interested in basketball, running, or anything like that. Lyle enjoys steer riding and roping. And Shane does woolly riding, or sheep riding. So Shane, Lyle, and Shannon really like the rodeo events, whereas my other two children, Warren and Joni, are more athletic. They are my runners and basketball players. We don't have soccer in our school yet, but I think that it would be nice if they did because it would be a lot of fun for the children.

My kids are always doing something. In the summertime we have lambs, the black-face lambs and the Suffolk lambs. The kids all participate in 4-H during the summer and get involved with 4-H projects. It keeps them busy all of the time. There is never a moment when they just relax and sit around. As I said, my children are always busy doing something.

Like many American families, Marilyn and her children are "on the go" most of the time. But there are other similarities. In addition to attending traditional Navajo ceremonies, Marilyn and her family also celebrate national holidays recognized by the federal government. She describes their participation and thoughts about these events.

Since our schools acknowledge national holidays, so do we. We respect the school and its teaching. We have Christmas at our house. At one time, our people did not know anything about Christmas. During the Long Walk and Fort Sumner days, none of us knew about Christmas. My grandmother did not ever really know the meaning of Christmas before she passed away, although she always knew that it was in December. Now our people know about it, and they love it because of the Christmas gifts that you can send. We decorate a tree and use the same decorations each year.

My kids also enjoy Easter because the school is really stressing that holiday. One thing I found out about, though, this past year was that when I taught my Navajo studies class, some parents complained. They said that their children are Christians and that they did not want them to learn about the traditional Navajo way. But I told them and other teachers that if we include Halloween, Christmas, and Easter in the school curriculum, then we must also teach the Navajo way of learning, reading, and writing. It is our way of life and the way that our people have always lived. I told them that if you live the Navajo cultural way, you respect your surroundings and yourself. I think that our way is even stricter than Christianity because we live it every day instead of just one day a week when you go to church.

My children also think that Halloween is fun. I take them trick or treating to a housing area where a lot of Diné people live. I personally do not like Halloween. I prefer my kids to dress up like a rabbit or something that is not scary like skeletons or ghosts. They have too much of an association with Navajo skin walkers or witches. I know that skin walkers exist, but I do not *believe* in them.

Many Diné believe that there are powerful witches, such as skin walkers, living on the Navajo Nation. A skin walker collects things from a person's home and gives these items to people who perform witchcraft. Other types of witches collect a person's hair, pieces of clothing, and even spit from the person's mouth. That is why Diné parents admonish their children to take care of themselves. If personal objects are left lying around, they can be gathered and used in an evil way against that person. After a Navajo encounters a witch, the medicine person conducts a Hózhǫ́ǫ́jí, Beautyway, to restore balance and harmony for the patient.

The Navajo belief in skin walkers or evil beings illustrates some of the challenges Marilyn undergoes to maintain balance and harmony, hózhǫ́, in her world. And through it all, she tries to uphold the traditional role of a woman in Navajo culture.

The role of women is important in Navajo culture because of the puberty ceremony (Kinaaldá) performed for White Shell Woman (Changing Woman). A woman is respected because she is the main root of the family. She is the one who bears the children, she is the one who gives life to the children. Therefore, she is respected for that. I guess that this is her main role. She is respected like Changing Woman and White Shell Woman because she is the one who has the children.

The mother usually tries to keep the home together because she is the one who cooks and does the weaving and keeps the fireplace going. The fire is very important to us because it is one of

the sacred elements. And so the woman is the one who is always taking care of the food, building a fire, and keeping harmony in the home, whereas the man does his work outside. He cannot be inside all of the time.

The mother must also take care of the children. She has to teach them, too. But the father also has a role because he identifies with the sun, Father Sun. In our culture they say that Father Sun is very harsh. That is the same way a man is. It is like men have the instinct of an animal that can get upset and mad. Men have a lot of power because of that instinct. The father is also very powerful and effective with his teaching. He will get his family together and talk to them about life and its values.

A woman's role in the home is to weave, take care of the food, take care of the fire, and keep the harmony.

Marilyn explains various techniques to her children about how to keep harmony between themselves and nature. She also shares the traditional Navajo strictures and taboos that influence their behavior.

I tell my children that they have to speak with good words. They cannot talk in any old way and make fun of people. I tell them to take care of their hair and to take care of themselves. I say, "Don't go and throw your things around, like your clothes, because you have got to learn how to take care of your things, especially your hair. You cannot just leave it anywhere." My grandmother used to get after me because sometimes I would leave my hair in a little bundle here or there. She would really get after me.

Our people celebrate our children's first laugh, too. The baby and the person who made them laugh give a feast. Everyone who attends the celebration party gets something to eat and partakes of the salt. We put rock salt, salt that is not iodized, in a Navajo basket, and then the baby, with the help of the person who made the baby laugh, gives each person a little bit of the salt and a bag of goodies. We do this so that a child will not be stingy for the rest of his or her life. We want the child to grow up to be a giving person.

We also say that if a coyote crosses your path, you have to know which direction he is going because if it is going a certain way, like the north, then it is bad. And if you hear an owl in the evening, it is bad, too. But if you hear the owl early in the morning, they say that it is good.

I tell my children to respect thunder and lightning because they are powerful and alive. When they hear thunder, they cannot be walking or running around because the thunder gets mad. They say that the male rain is the one with the really heavy water and the darkest clouds. The female rain is the one that barely comes down and is gentle. But when there is lots of lightning and

thunder that comes down here and there, here and there, we say that the lightning and thunder are the children trying out their thunder and their lightning bolts. That is why you have to respect them and talk to them, too.

Contemporary material goods are also evident throughout the Navajo Nation. For example, trucks have replaced horses, even for the Help family.

We have a truck because we have to do a lot of work hauling hay and hauling water. There is a lot of stuff that we have to do. We go up to the mountains and haul wood with it in the fall. We also go up to the mine and haul coal. Our truck is used all of the time for all sorts of things. Sometimes we even haul poles. So that is why we really need a truck. The last time I got a vehicle, I really wanted to buy this nice van, but I had to weigh out the reasons. I knew I couldn't get the van for where we live, so that's why I ended up getting a truck again.

Marilyn also gets involved with Navajo politics on the local level. The Navajo Nation is divided into districts, and each one has a chapter house with elected leaders. She discusses their function and various hot topics such as the issues of gambling and women's leadership.

I try to get involved with our chapter house because that is where I need to be so that my voice can be heard. It seems like nowadays the people perceive our chapter as only helping certain people and not helping everyone. So some of our people don't want to go to the meetings. The younger people don't want to go there, so it is only the older people who attend. But if we are going to discuss an important issue, it is important for the younger people to be there so they will know what is going on and can be a part of it. This is not what is being done now.

Most of the chapter presidents are men. I asked my dad about it and whether or not it is right for a woman to be the Navajo Nation president or a chapter house president. My dad said that he doesn't think it is right for a woman to be a leader because the men are always the warriors and make the decisions. He explained that in our traditional way the twins (Monster Slayer and Child Born of Water) conquered the monsters. Therefore, he said that you have to leave it to men to do the planning. But I think that women make a lot of the decisions in the home and often make sense when they are talking. Their opinions are respected, too. I have noticed that there are more councilwomen now than there used to be.

I think that most of our people are against gambling. But there are younger people and council people who really want it. We voted on it once and said that we do not want gambling

Figure 12
Manuelito in Costume, War Chief of the Navajos, New Mexico. Courtesy of the National Museum of the American Indian, Smithsonian Institution, neg. no. N37814. Photographer unknown.

and we don't want alcohol to be legalized. It will change our lives if we vote for gambling because our people may go into town and spend their money away once a month when they get paid. Many of our council people are talking about this issue. This is why it is important to go to chapter meetings so that we can discuss issues like this.

This chapter gives a portrayal of the

contemporary Navajo world from the viewpoint of a woman and her family who successfully live the traditional Diné way side by side with the surrounding majority culture. They celebrate their identity by participating in sacred ceremonies, praying to the Holy People, raising and herding livestock, respecting time-honored customs, living among the four sacred mountains, and speaking their native tongue. Marilyn Help and her family are proud of their heritage and identity: the Diné, the People, the Navajo.

The Song Connection

Traditional and contemporary music are juxtaposed constantly in the Navajo world. Although Marilyn embraces the music of her past that is handed down by oral tradition from her elders, she also enjoys and values music from the present. "Go, My Son" is a song that touches her heart because its message encourages young people to get an education. She frequently sings this song and "signs" the words for both Navajo and non-Navajo audiences.

"Go, My Son"

Background Information

"Go, My Son" is originally by Arlene Nofchissey Williams and Carnes Burson. I guess they wrote it when they were at Brigham Young University. Ever since it was written, it has been something that my people can relate to. Our people thought that Chief Manuelito made a lot of good decisions, so they asked him for his advice about what was going to happen. Manuelito told the council, "I want our children to go ahead and get educated. That is the only way that our people will be able to know. That is the only way our people will live a life in both worlds. That is our only way to get back what has been taken from us. Our children must get educated so that they can have the same mind as the white people. That is the only way we can fight for ourselves now. We have to have our children get education so that they can survive in both worlds." The people respected what he said, and so that is why this song came about. When Arlene Nofchissey Williams and Carnes Burson were interviewed, this is exactly what they said. They said that they dedicated this song to Chief Manuelito because he was the one who really stressed that education was like a ladder to help our people. And so that is why they made this song. Our people can really relate to this song because it means a lot. The lyrics really make our children think. When I teach it in my classes, I have it written down. I always ask them what they think this means, to "go and earn your feather." They think about it and do a lot of critical thinking. They have a lot of ideas about what it means. I teach this song with hand motions, and they really enjoy them. (see Figure 12)

Note: The "signing" hand motions that Marilyn performs with this song are described in Appendix E.

Go, My Son

Words and Music by
Carnes Burson and
Arlene Nofchissey Williams
Used by permission

Epilogue

When Marilyn came to my home for the last review of this book, we laughed spontaneously and joyously as we exchanged the latest stories of our lives with each other. But in addition to our laughter, singing, and dancing, a special event occurred: Marilyn shared her prayers to the Holy People with me. She had this inspiration during our recording session when she showed me her sacred corn pollen bag for the very first time. On an impulse, Marilyn excitedly suggested that we bless our project in the traditional Diné way that uses corn pollen as part of the ritual. I quickly agreed with her idea. We went outside my front door, which faces east, and looked at the mountains glowing in the late afternoon sunshine. She took a small amount of corn pollen in her hand and placed it in her mouth and on the top of her head, after which she gestured four times to the east. Marilyn then asked me to perform the same prayer, which I did with great reverence and respect. Several weeks later, when I visited her at her home in Tolakai, we held the rough draft of the book and blessed it in similar fashion. I was deeply moved by these events because I felt the power of our friendship, the true meaning of cultural diversity, and most important, the presence of the Holy People.

Marilyn's prayers to the Holy People and her belief in them reflects the spirit of *We'll Be in Your Mountains, We'll Be in Your Songs: A Navajo Woman Sings*. This book was written to promote cultural understanding and deep respect for cultural differences. The authors sincerely hope that the Holy People bless and support this project.

With this spirit of cooperation and goodwill, we encourage readers to honor the performance time strictures for each song and dance that we share in this book. To do so is to honor the Navajo. Marilyn passionately believes in the power of the Holy People and the beauty of the songs and dances of the Diné.

Our traditional way of living, our religion, reflects the teachings of the Holy People. They say that before the Holy People left, they taught the Diné everything about life and what it is going to be like. In a way, they gave us the "ten commandments" to live by. When they were ready to leave, they said, "We'll be in your mountains, we'll be in your songs. That's the way to remember us. We'll be in your symbols. That's how you will remember us and our teachings so that you may have a good life." And that is how we remember them and their instructions. We remember them through our stories and through our songs.

Appendix A

THE NAVAJO LANGUAGE

The Diné believe that the Holy People gave them the gift of their native tongue, Navajo. It is a tonal language that reflects the subtle nuances of high and low vocal pitches. In addition, glottal stops and nasalized tone colors are characteristic sounds of their speech. Cultural outsiders describe the Navajo language as being "challenging." Indeed, the very fact that the Navajo language is complex was used advantageously during World War II. It was the basis of a secret code used by Navajo marines to communicate urgent confidential messages to their fellow soldiers and allies. As hard as the Japanese tried, they could not decipher the code. Locke states:

Navajos fought in every theater of the war and the military commanders soon discovered that they could perform a unique service. Their complex language was completely unknown to the enemy and was ideal as a means of sending messages, in place of sending codes. A platoon of Navajo "code talkers" served throughout the Pacific campaign and the Japanese could not break the perplexing "code" that never ceased to confuse them. The Japanese were willing to pay riches to any Navajo willing to defect and teach them the language. (Locke 1992, 449)

Several books and videos document the Navajo Codetalkers and their contribution to the United States victory in World War II. Their unique language was a key component in their success.

Marilyn values her native language and encourages her own children to speak and write it. Because Marilyn communicates exclusively in Navajo to her youngest son, Shane, he speaks and understands his "mother tongue" better than his siblings do.

Language is very sacred. Remember when we had the first laugh? It is the beginning of speech. That is why we have the first laugh celebration.

Everyone has this speech. When our Navajo language is gone, we will all be common. The Holy People gave us our eyes and our mouth for a purpose. The Holy People gave us these things. They said do not be harsh when you speak. Our lips and our tongues are sacred. They are like lightning when we speak, from the East, South, West, and North.

There is lightning in our mouths, and we must take care of what we say.

Some people do not appreciate our language. I want our people to relearn Navajo if they have lost it. I want them to read it, to write it, and to speak it.

The best way to learn the Navajo language is to listen to it and then practice it repeatedly.

Pronunciation Guide for the Navajo Language

This information is taken directly from the *Conversational Navajo Dictionary*, by Garth A. Wilson.

Navajo	English	Navajo	English	Navajo	English
b	*boy*	*s*	*so*	*y*	*yes*
d	*door*	*z*	*zoo*	*a*	*father*
t	*time*	*sh*	*she*	*e*	*let*
k	*kite*	*zh*	*pleasure*	*i*	*bit*
kw	*quick*	*ts*	*hats*	*o*	*go*
g	*go*	*m*	*mad*	*ee*	*they*
ch	*chair*	*n*	*not*	*ii*	*see*
j	*joy*	*l*	*like*		
h	*have*	*w*	*wood*	(Wilson 1994,2)	

"Navajo vowels (and the consonant *n*) can take on either of two tones—high or low. The high tone is indicated by a 'high mark' (') over the letter" (ibid., 5).

"A nasal mark (˛) under a vowel indicates that it is nasalized. A vowel with no nasal mark is oral" (ibid., 7).

The consonant *ł* may be pronounced in a breathy manner. "Place your tongue in a position as if to make an 'l' sound. Then blow out" (ibid., 8).

The Navajo language also uses a glottal stop. "Sound made by stopping the air with the glottis as in 'oh'oh,' 'butler' (bu'ler), or 'hu', two, three, four!'" (ibid., 10).

Note: A highly recommended source for Navajo language study is *Diné Bizaad: Speak, Read, Write Navajo*, by Irvy W. Goossen (see the bibliography).

Appendix B

MOTIONS FOR THE SONG "SHÍ NAASHÁ"

Shí	Point to yourself and touch your fingers on your chest with both hands.
naashá ghạ	Point outward with your palms facing upward.
Lago hózhǫ́ǫ́ lá, hee ya hee nee ya'.	Clap your hands together on each beat.
Ládéé hózhǫ́ǫ́ lá, hee ya hee nee ya'.	Clap your hands together on each beat.
Ahala ahalágó naashá ghạ.	Put your hands in front of you with your fingertips pointing toward each other, almost touching. Your palms face inward toward your chest. Move your palms in a circular motion, outward at the top and inward at the bottom. Both hands move exactly together. Move your hands through two complete cycles.

Appendix C

MOTIONS TO THE SONG "NÁÁ' DIISHOH"

Try grinding corn using the corn-grinding equipment of the metate, larger stone (*tsé deeshjee'*), and mano, smaller stone (*tsé deeshch'įní*). Or perform the motions using "air" movements to feel the beat and flow of the song.

Motion A: Move your arms back and forth to the beat of the song; grind the corn in a traditional way using two stones. Place the corn on the larger stone, the metate, and press down on the corn with the smaller stone, the mano.

Motion B: When you hear the word *náá'diishoh*, sweep off the corn with a brush and continue brushing until Motion A occurs again.

Ee yaheya, ee yaheya,	Motion A	*Háásh díítłíílgo saał ník'áó,*	Motion A
Haloo shee yee weeseloo,		*wee ya he',*	
Haloo shee yee weeseloo weeseloo,		*Eyaheyahe aa'a' awe awe.*	
Haloo shee yee weeselaa,		*Yoo'oo náá'diishoh,*	Motion B
'Oo wee 'oo wo		*yoo'oo náá'diishoh,*	
'Ee yee náá'diishoh,	Motion B	*Yoo'oo, tsxį́įłgo*	Motion A
Eyaheyahe aa' a' awe awe.		*nik'ao wee yaa he',*	
Awéé' yichaoo, awéé'	Motion A	*Eyaheyahe aa' a' awe awe.*	
yichaoo, awéé' yichaoo,		*Haloo shee yee weeseloo,*	Motion A
Yoo'oo náá'diishoh,	Motion B	*haloo shee yee*	
yoo'oo náá'diishoh,		*Weeseloo weeseloo,*	
Tsxį́įłgo ník'áó	Motion A	*Haloo shee yee weeseloo,*	
wee yaa he',		*'Oo wee 'oo wo 'ee*	
Eyaheyahe aa'		*yee náá'diishoh,*	Motion B
a' awe awe.		*Eyaheyahe aa' a' awe awe.*	

Appendix D

MOTIONS FOR THE SONG "KIIZH"

Bíjáá' nei diłdiłgóó
(He flops his ears)

Arm Position: Put your R hand close to the side of your R ear but not touching; put your L hand close to the side of your L ear but not touching; palms face outward.

Arm Movement: Move your R and L hands up and down rapidly, like dog ears.

Bítséé' nei diłtas
(He wags his tail)

Arm Position: Put your R arm by your R side with palms and fingers facing inward toward your body.

Arm Movement: Move your R hand and arm swiftly and rapidly in an inward and outward motion toward your body.

T'áá akwííjįį bibid neishood
(Every day he drags his belly around)

Arm Position: Put your R and L hands in front of your body, with fingertips touching, slightly below waist level.

Arm Movement: Cradle your hands back and forth.

Appendix E

MOTIONS FOR THE SONG "GO, MY SON"

Go, my

Arm Position: Bend your R elbow with your R forearm pointing upward, parallel to the body; face your R palm forward with your four fingers touching; point your thumb to the left at a forty-five-degree angle to your fingers. Unless otherwise indicated, your L arm is in a relaxed position at your L side.

Movement: Push your R palm and R forearm forward, extending the whole arm, as if pushing something away, dipping slightly, then rising; then return your arm to the original position.

son

Arm Position: Bend your R elbow with your R forearm parallel to the body; point your R index finger upward while holding your other fingers and thumb close together; relax your R hand.

Movement: Push your R index finger, R hand, and R forearm forward, extending the whole arm, as if pushing something away, dipping slightly, then rising; then return your arm to the original position.

Go and climb the ladder

Arm Position: Bend both elbows and bring both forearms in front of your chest, parallel to the floor and to each other, one on top of each other but not touching.

Movement: Rotate your hands and forearms around each other without touching and move them in an upward, vertical direction, as if climbing a ladder.

Go my

Same as before.

son

Same as before.

Go and earn your

Arm Position: Make a "feather" with your R index and middle finger touching and pointing upward; touch your other fingers and thumb together in front.

Movement: Put the "feather" behind the top of your head so that it can still be seen.

feather

Arm Position: Same as preceding.

Movement: Move your "feather" finger formation forward to the front R side of your body with a dip movement that ends up at your eye level with your arm fully extended at the end of the motion.

Go my

Same as before.

son

Same as before.

Make your people proud of

Arm Position: Face your L palm toward your R side with your L arm up and your L elbow bent; hold your fingers straight up and touching with the L thumb at a forty-five-degree angle to the back; put your R forearm in front of your body and parallel to the floor at chest level, palm down; hold your R hand fingers and thumb together.

Movement: Hold your L arm still and, keeping your R arm in front of you at chest level, point your R hand fingers downward to an imaginary spot to the R front, then, with your R arm, cross your midline and point to an imaginary spot at the L front, as if you are moving an object on an imaginary table.

you

Arm Position: Leave your L arm stationary in the position described above; begin this motion with the R arm and hand where they left off from the last step.

Movement: Make a rainbow motion with the R arm, starting from the L at chest level, and move to the R side; move your fingers throughout the rainbow motion as if making raindrops.

Work, my son

Arm Position: Face your R and L palms toward each other in front of your midline, fingers pointing forward and parallel to the floor.

Movement: Move your R and L palms upward and downward in a relaxed manner, alternating directions with each other, as if the hands are wiping each other, but not touching.

Get an education

Arm Position: Face both palms toward the floor, side by side, in front of the body between the waist and chest level.

Movement: Gracefully turn your palms over so that they are facing upward, touching like a book.

Work, my son

Same as before.

Learn a good vocation

Arm Position: Put your R hand to your R side with your palm facing upward. Put your L arm with the L elbow bent in front of your body at waist level with your L palm facing upward.

Movement: Bring your R palm back to midline, parallel with your waist and with the R palm remaining up, slightly above the L palm. Your left arm remains stationary.

And climb, my son

Arm Position: Bend both elbows and bring both forearms in front of your chest, parallel to the floor and to each other, one on top of each other but not touching.

Movement: Rotate your hands and forearms around each other without touching and move them in an upward, vertical direction, as if climbing a ladder.

Go and take a lofty view

Arm Position: Bend your R elbow with your R forearm parallel to the body and pointing upward; face your R palm outward with your fingers extended upward.

Movement: Slowly wave your R hand and move it gradually to the R; continue waving in a "beauty pageant contestant" fashion.

Oo-oo-oo- . . .

During the interlude, twirl your hands to the left in a parallel circular motion, like a waterwheel, then open both hands with both palms facing upward at the end of the phrase. Then do the same movement pattern to the right. This sequence is performed to the L, R, L, R, and L.

From on the ladder

Arm Position: Bend both elbows and bring both forearms in front of your chest, parallel to the floor and to each other, one on top of each other but not touching.

Movement: Rotate your hands and forearms around each other without touching and move them in an upward, vertical direction, as if climbing a ladder.

Of an education

Arm Position: Face both palms toward the floor, side by side, in front of the body between the waist and chest level.

Movement: Turn your palms over so that they are facing upward, touching like a book.

You can see to

Arm Position: Put your R hand on your forehead with your palm facing downward, as if shading your eyes from the sun.

Movement: Look outward with your hand on your forehead and pretend to see something in the distance.

Help your Indian nation

Arm Position: Touch your R hand fingers and thumb at chest level.

Movement: Move your R hand away from your body in a continuous, horizontal, zigzag motion with your fingers and thumb pointing downward, as if you are etching a zigzag design on a table.

And reach, my son

Arm Position: Put your R hand and forearm in front of your body at chest level with your palm facing up.

Movement: Slowly move your R arm to the R, going upward.

And lift your people up with you

Arm Position: Face your R and L palms toward your body at chest level with your fingertips almost touching.

Movement: Extend your hands and arms forward, palms facing upward, slowly rising, as if asking an audience to rise.

(D.C. al fine)

Selected Bibliography

Adair, John. *The Navajo and Pueblo Silversmiths.* Norman: University of Oklahoma Press, 1989.

Bailey, L. R. *The Long Walk: A History of the Navajo Wars, 1846–68.* Tucson, Ariz.: Westernlore Press, 1988.

Begay, Shonto. *Navajo Visions and Voices Across the Mesa.* New York: Scholastic, Inc., 1995.

Bennett, Kay and Russ. *A Navajo Saga.* San Antonio, Texas: The Naylor Company, 1972.

Brugge, David M. "Navajo Prehistory and History to 1850." In *Handbook of North American Indians,* vol. 10: *Southwest,* edited by Alfonso Ortiz. Washington, D.C.: Smithsonian Institution, 1983.

Duncan, Lois. *The Magic of Spider Woman.* New York: Scholastic, Inc., 1996.

Goossen, Irvy W. *Diné Bizaad: Speak, Read, Write Navajo.* Flagstaff, Ariz.: Solina Bookshelf, 1995.

Iverson, Peter. *The Navajos.* New York: Chelsea House Publishers, 1990.

Johnson, Broderick, H., ed. *Navajo Stories of the Long Walk Period.* Tsaile, Navajo Nation, Ariz.: Navajo Community College Press, 1973.

Johnson (Frisbie), Charlotte I. "Navajo Corn Grinding Songs." *Ethnomusicology* 8 (May 1964): 101–20.

Kluckhohn, Clyde, W. W. Hill, and Lucy Wales Kluckhohn. *Navaho Material Culture.* Cambridge, Mass.: The Belknap Press of Harvard University Press, 1971.

Kluckhohn, Clyde, and Dorothea Leighton. *The Navajo.* Cambridge, Mass.: Harvard University Press, 1974.

Locke, Raymond Friday. *The Book of the Navajo.* Los Angeles: Mankind Publishing Company, 1992.

Lynch, Regina H. *A History of Navajo Clans.* Rough Rock, Ariz.: Navajo Curriculum Center, 1993.

McAllester, David P. *Enemy Way Music.* Cambridge, Mass.: Harvard University Printing Office, 1954.

———. *Indian Music in the Southwest.* Colorado Springs, Colo.: Taylor Museum of the Colorado Springs Fine Arts Center, 1961.

———. "North America/Native America." In *Worlds of Music,* edited by Jeff Titon. New York: Schirmer, 1992.

———. "North American Native Music." In *Musics of Many Cultures,* edited by Elizabeth May. Berkeley: University of California Press, 1980.

McAllester, David P., and Douglas F. Mitchell. "Navajo Music." In *Handbook of North American Indians,* vol. 10: *Southwest,* edited by Alfonso Ortiz. Washington, D.C.: Smithsonian Institution, 1983.

Navajo Curriculum Center. *A History of Navajo Clans.* Chinle, Ariz.: Navajo Curriculum Center, Rough Rock Demonstration School, 1993.

O'Bryan, Aileen. *Navajo Indian Myths.* New York: Dover Publications, Inc., 1993.

Parnwell, E. C. *The New Oxford Picture Dictionary: English/Navajo Edition.* England: Oxford University Press, 1989.

Reichard, Gladys. *Spider Woman: A Story of Navajo Weavers and Chanters.* Glorieta, N.M.: The Rio Grande Press, Inc., 1968.

Rhodes, Willard, ed. *Music of the American Indian: Navajo.* Library of Congress, AFS L41. Accompanying recording notes, 1987.

———, ed. *Music of the Sioux and the Navajo*. Ethnic Folkways Library, RE 4401. Accompanying recording notes, 1953.

Roessel, Monty. *Kinaaldá: A Navajo Girl Grows Up*. Minneapolis: Lerner Publication Company, 1993.

Roessel, Robert A., Jr. *Navajo Arts and Crafts*. Rough Rock, Ariz.: Navajo Curriculum Center, Rough Rock Demonstration School, 1983.

———. *Pictorial History of the Navajo from 1860–1910*. Rough Rock, Ariz.: Navajo Curriculum Center, Rough Rock Demonstration School, 1980.

Roessel, Ruth. "Navajo Arts and Crafts." In *Handbook of North American Indians*, vol. 10: *Southwest*, edited by Alfonso Ortiz. Washington, D.C.: Smithsonian Institution, 1983.

———. *Women in Navajo Society*. Rough Rock, Ariz.: Navajo Resource Center, Rough Rock Demonstration School, 1981.

Roessel, Ruth, and Broderick H. Johnson. *Navajo Livestock Reduction: A National Disgrace*. Chinle, Ariz.: Navajo Community College Press, 1974.

Sundberg, Lawrence D. *Dinetah: An Early History of the Navajo People*. Santa Fe, N.M.: Sunstone Press, 1995.

Title IV-B Materials Development Project. *Navajo Art, History and Culture*. Rough Rock, Ariz.: Navajo Curriculum Center, Rough Rock Demonstration School, 1984.

Underhill, Ruth M. *The Navajos*. Norman: University of Oklahoma Press, 1956.

Wilson, Alan. *Navajo Place Names*. Guilford, Conn.: Jeffrey Norton Publishers, 1995.

Wilson, Garth A. *Conversational Navajo Dictionary: English to Navajo*. Blanding, Utah: Conversational Navajo Publications, 1990.

Witherspoon, Gary. "Language and Reality in Navajo World View." In *Handbook of North American Indians*, vol. 10: *Southwest*, edited by Alfonso Ortiz. Washington, D.C.: Smithsonian Institution, 1983.

Wyman, Leland C. "Navajo Ceremonial System." In *Handbook of North American Indians*, vol. 10: *Southwest*, edited by Alfonso Ortiz. Washington, D.C.: Smithsonian Institution, 1983.

Yazzie, Dollie L. *Navajo Music for Classroom Enrichment*. Chinle, Ariz.: Navajo Curriculum Center, Rough Rock Demonstration School, 1976.

Yazzie, Ethelou. *Navajo History*. Chinle, Ariz.: Rough Rock Press, 1971.

Selected Discography

Kaibah. Kay Bennett. KB 6667.

Music of the American Indian: Navajo. The Library of Congress. AFS L41.

Music of the Sioux and the Navajo. Ethnic Folkways Library. RE 4401.

Navajo Corn Grinding Songs. Indian House. IH 1507.

Navajo Gift Songs. Indian House. IH 1505.

Navajo Music for Classroom Enrichment. Navajo Curriculum Center, Rough Rock Demonstration School, Chinle, Ariz.

Navajo Nation Swingers: Navajo Style. Sound of America Records, Albuquerque, N.M. SOAR-123.

Navajo Peyote Songs, vols. 1–4. Indian House. IH 1541-4.

Navajo Round Dance. Indian House. IH 1504.

Navajo Skip Dance & Two-Step Songs. Indian House. IH 1503.

Navajo Songs About Love, #1–6. Indian House. IH 1509-14.

Navajo Sway Songs. Indian House. IH 1501.

Night and Daylight Yei-Be-Chai. Indian House. IH 1502.

R. Carlos Nakai: Changes. Canyon Records Productions. CR-615.

Sharon Burch, Yazzie Girl. Canyon Records Productions. CR-534.

Songs from the Navajo Nation by Kaibah. Kay Bennett. KB 4172B.

Sweethearts of Navajoland: Navajo Traditional Two-Step and Skip Songs. Canyon Records Productions. CR-7160.

Traditional Navajo Songs. Canyon Records Productions. CR-6064.

Worlds of Music. Schirmer Books. ISBN 0-02-872601-4.

Sources for Recordings

Canyon Records Productions. 4143 North Sixteenth Street, Suite 6, Phoenix, Ariz. 85016. (800) 268-1141.

Ethnic Folkways Library. (Now housed at the Smithsonian Institution. See Smithsonian/Folkways listing.)

Indian House. Box 472, Taos, N.M. 87571. (505) 776-2953.

Library of Congress. Archives of Folk Culture, Motion Picture, Broadcast, and Recorded Sound Division, Library of Congress, Washington, D.C. 20540. (202) 707-7833.

Navajo Curriculum Center. Rough Rock Demonstration School, Rough Rock, Ariz. 86503.

Smithsonian/Folkways. The Folkways Collection, Smithsonian Institution, Washington, D.C. 20560. (202) 287-3262.

Sound of America Records (SOAR). PO Box 8606, Albuquerque, N.M. 87198. (505) 268-6110.

Selected Videos

Navajo. American Indian Video Series. Tellens, Inc., 1982.

Navajo Code Talkers: The Epic Story. Tully Entertainment, 1995.

Sandpainting: A Navajo Tradition. INTERpark, 1990.

Seasons of the Navajo. PBS 275, 1988.

Sources for Videos

INTERpark. 1540 E. McArthur, Cortez, Colo. 81321.

Public Broadcasting System. 1320 Braddock Place, Alexandria, Va. 22314-1698.

Tellens, Inc. Museum of Northern Arizona. 3101 N. Fort Valley Rd., Flagstaff, Ariz. 86001. (520) 774-5213.

Tully Entertainment. 1-800-247-6553.

Notes